Information Technology and Law Series

Volume 28

More information about this series at http://www.springer.com/series/8857

Rowena Rodrigues · Vagelis Papakonstantinou
Editors

Privacy and Data Protection Seals

ASSER PRESS

Springer

Editors
Rowena Rodrigues
Trilateral Research Ltd.
London
UK

Vagelis Papakonstantinou
Law, Science, Technology &
  Society Studies (LSTS)
VUB (Vrije Universiteit Brussel)
Brussels
Belgium

ISSN 1570-2782   ISSN 2215-1966   (electronic)
Information Technology and Law Series
ISBN 978-94-6265-227-9   ISBN 978-94-6265-228-6   (eBook)
https://doi.org/10.1007/978-94-6265-228-6

Library of Congress Control Number: 2017957693

Published by T.M.C. ASSER PRESS, The Hague, The Netherlands www.asserpress.nl
Produced and distributed for T.M.C. ASSER PRESS by Springer-Verlag Berlin Heidelberg

Printed on acid-free paper

This T.M.C.ASSER PRESS imprint is published by the registered company Springer-Verlag GmbH, DE part
of Springer Nature
The registered company address is: Heidelberger Platz 3, 14197 Berlin, Germany

Series Information

The *Information Technology & Law Series* was an initiative of ITeR, the national programme for Information Technology and Law, which was a research programme set up by the Dutch government and The Netherlands Organisation for Scientific Research (NWO) in The Hague. Since 1995 ITeR has published all of its research results in its own book series. In 2002 ITeR launched the present internationally orientated and English language *Information Technology & Law Series*. This well-established series deals with the implications of information technology for legal systems and institutions. Manuscripts and related correspondence can be sent to the Series' Editorial Office, which will also gladly provide more information concerning editorial standards and procedures.

Editorial Office

T.M.C. Asser Instituut
P.O. Box 30461
2500 GL The Hague
The Netherlands
Tel.: +31-70-3420300
e-mail: itandlaw@asser.nl

Simone van der Hof, *Editor-in-Chief*
Leiden University, eLaw (Center for Law and Digital Technologies)
The Netherlands

Bibi van den Berg
Leiden University, eLaw (Center for Law and Digital Technologies)
The Netherlands

Eleni Kosta
Tilburg University, TILT (Tilburg Institute for Law, Technology and Society)
The Netherlands

Ulrich Sieber
Max Planck Institute for Foreign and International Criminal Law
Freiburg
Germany

Contents

Editors and Contributors

About the Editors

Rowena Rodrigues, Ph.D. is Senior Research Analyst at Trilateral Research, UK. Her areas of expertise and research interests include privacy and data protection (law, policy, and practice), privacy certification, security and surveillance, comparative legal analysis, regulation of new technologies, ethics and governance of new and emerging technologies, and responsible research & innovation. She has published chapters in books by Springer, Routledge, Policy Press, and articles in journals such as the *Computer Law & Security Review, European Journal of Social Science Research, International Data Privacy Law*, and *the Journal of Contemporary European Research.* At Trilateral, she has contributed/contributes in various capacities to EU-funded research projects (e.g. EU Privacy Seals Project, IRISS, PULSE, SATORI) and provides consultancy to the private sector. Rowena has a Ph.D. in law from the University of Edinburgh.

Vagelis Papakonstantinou is a legal scholar in Brussels, Belgium, where he works as a senior researcher at the Vrije Universiteit Brussel, and a practicing attorney in Athens, Greece, where he co-founded and runs MPlegal, a law firm. Since 2016, he serves as a member (alternate) of the Hellenic Data Protection Authority. Personal website: http://www.papakonstantinou.me/.

Contributors

Prof. Dr. Paolo Balboni (qualified lawyer admitted to the Milan Bar and Lead Auditor BS ISO/IEC 27001:2013 - IRCA Certified) is a founding partner of ICT Legal Consulting (ICTLC), a law firm with offices in Milan, Bologna, Rome, an international desk in Amsterdam, and multiple partner law firms around the world. Together with his team, he advises clients in the field of personal data protection, and acts as Data Protection Officer in outsourcing, data security, Information and Communication Technology (ICT) and Intellectual Property Law. Paolo has considerable experience in Information Technologies including cloud computing, big data, analytics and the Internet of Things, media and entertainment, healthcare, fashion, automotive, insurance, banking, Anti-Money Laundering (AML) and Counter-Terrorist Financing (CFT). Paolo is Professor of Privacy, Cybersecurity, and IT Contract Law at the European Centre on Privacy and Cybersecurity (ECPC) within the Maastricht University Faculty of Law; President of the European Privacy

Association based in Brussels; Cloud Computing Sector Director; and Responsible for Foreign Affairs at the Italian Institute for Privacy in Rome, Italy. He is involved in European Commission studies on new technologies and participated in the revision of the EU Commission proposal for a General Data Protection Regulation. Paolo is the author of the book 'Trustmarks in E-Commerce: The Value of Web Seals and the Liability of their Providers' (T.M.C Asser Press), and numerous journal articles published in leading European law reviews.

Dr. David Barnard-Wills is a Senior Research Analyst at Trilateral Research. His research and policy analysis expertise include the politics of surveillance and security, cyber security, online privacy, identity technology, terrorism and counter-terrorism resilience, decision support, and certification. He was previously a Research Fellow in the Department of Informatics and Systems Engineering at Cranfield University, Defence Academy of the United Kingdom, the School of Political Science and International Studies at the University of Birmingham and for the Parliamentary Office of Science and Technology. He has a Ph.D. in Politics and an M.A. in Political Science from the University of Nottingham. For Trilateral, he has led projects on societal impact of security research (www.assert-project.eu), European perceptions of privacy and surveillance (www.prismsproject.eu), and international cooperation between data protection authorities (www.phaedra-project.eu). He has also contributed to studies for the EU Joint Research Centre on privacy seals and for DG Connect on certification schemes for cloud computing. He was the lead for Trilateral on the ENISA *Threat Landscape and Good Practice Guide for Smart Home and Converged Media*. He has published 16 peer-reviewed articles in academic journals as well as chapters, reviews, and reports.

Johanna Carvais-Palut (after a year with a law firm) worked for ten years at the French Data Protection Authority (CNIL). Her first appointment at CNIL was as a legal adviser in the economic affairs department. While at CNIL, she created the Privacy Seal Unit and oversaw it for four years. She is currently a data protection officer in Malakoff Mederic (an insurance company) and leads its GDPR compliance project. She has written many articles and presented at data protection events.

Dr. Ann Cavoukian is recognised as one of the world's leading privacy experts. She is presently the Executive Director of the Privacy and Big Data Institute at Ryerson University. She served an unprecedented three terms as the Information & Privacy Commissioner of Ontario, Canada. There, she created Privacy by Design (PbD), a framework that seeks to proactively embed privacy into design, thereby achieving the strongest protection possible. In 2010, international privacy regulators unanimously passed a Resolution recognising PbD as an international standard. Since then, PbD has been translated into 39 languages. She has received numerous awards recognising her leadership in privacy, including being named as one of the *Top 25 Women of Influence in Canada*, named among the *Top 10 women in Data Security and Privacy*, and most recently, named as one of the *Top 100 Leaders in Identity* (January 2017).

Michelle Chibba is a Strategic Privacy/Policy Advisor at the Privacy and Big Data Institute at Ryerson University, Toronto, Ontario. She is a co-instructor along with Dr. Cavoukian, for the course on Privacy by Design: The Global Framework, the Chang School at Ryerson University. Prior to this, she was Director, Policy Department and Special Projects at the Office of the Information and Privacy Commissioner of Ontario, Canada (IPC).

Prof. Paul De Hert is a human rights and law & technology scholar working in constitutionalism, criminal law, and surveillance law. He is interested both in legal practice and more fundamental reflections about law. At the Vrije Universiteit Brussel (VUB), He holds the chair of "European Criminal Law". In the past, he has taught "Historical Constitutionalism", "Human Rights", "Legal theory", and "Constitutional criminal law". He is Director of the Research Group on Fundamental Rights and Constitutionalism (FRC), Director of the Department of Interdisciplinary Studies of Law (Metajuridics), and a co-director of the Research Group Law Science Technology & Society (LSTS). He is an associated professor at Tilburg University where he teaches "Privacy and Data Protection" at the Tilburg Institute of Law, Technology, and Society (TILT).

Theodora Dragan graduated from the Faculty of Laws of the University College London, where she studied Law with German Law. She spent a year abroad at the Ludwig-Maximilian University of Munich. During her studies, she focused on Intellectual Property Law and Data Protection. She was awarded 5th place at the International Alternative Dispute Resolution Tournament (2015). As a Fellow of the European Privacy Association, she led a series of webinars on the General Data Protection Regulation in 2016. She co-wrote the chapter on controversies and challenges of trustmarks together with Paolo Balboni, in her role as Associate at ICT Legal Consulting, the largest and most specialised data protection firm in Italy.

Marit Hansen is the State Data Protection Commissioner of Land Schleswig-Holstein, Germany, and Chief of Unabhängiges Landeszentrum für Datenschutz (ULD; in English: Independent Centre for Privacy Protection). Before being appointed Data Protection Commissioner in 2015, she was Deputy Commissioner for seven years. Within ULD, she established the "Privacy Technology Projects" Division and the "Innovation Centre Privacy & Security". Since her diploma in computer science in 1995, she has been working on privacy and security aspects. Her focus is "data protection by design" and "data protection by default" from both the technical and the legal perspectives.

Irene Kamara is a Ph.D. researcher at the Tilburg Institute for Law, Technology, and Society (TILT) at the Tilburg University in the Netherlands. She is also affiliate researcher at the Vrije Universiteit Brussel (LSTS). Her research interests include personal data protection, privacy, standardisation, conformity assessment, and Internet of Things. Prior to joining academia, she worked as an attorney at law before the Court of Appeal in Athens. She has collaborated with the European Data Protection Supervisor, the Research Executive Agency, CEN, and CENELEC. She is currently selected as a member of the ENISA Experts List for assisting in the implementation of the Annual ENISA Work Programme. She holds a LL.M. in Law and Technology from the University of Tilburg (cum laude), a M.Sc. in European and International Studies from the University of Piraeus (with distinction) and a LL.B. In 2015, she received a best paper award and a young author recognition certificate from the International Standardisation Union (ITU), the United Nations Agency for standardisation.

Patrick Waelbroeck is professor of industrial economics and econometrics at Telecom Paristech. He earned a Ph.D. in economics from the University of Paris 1 Panthéon-Sorbonne. He also holds a master degree from Yale University for which he obtained a Fulbright scholarship. His research and teaching focus on the economics of innovation, the economics of intellectual property, Internet economics, and the economics of personal data. He is a member of the editorial board of the Journal of Cultural Economics. He is area editor of Annals of Telecommunications. He is a member of the board of the international association European Policy for Intellectual Property. He was president of the association during 2013–2014. He is also a founding member of the Chair "Valeurs et Politiques des Informations Personnelles" (Values and Policies of Personal Information), Institut Mines-Télécom, that addresses legal, economic, technical, and philosophical issues related to personal data.

Chapter 1
Introduction: Privacy and Data Protection Seals

Vagelis Papakonstantinou

Abstract This chapter sets out some terminological guidance as well as the aims and scope of the book. It guides the reader through the structure and presents them with a flavor of the contents of the book.

Keywords privacy · privacy seals · data protection seals · certification · data protection

Certification and data privacy have a long, and at times strained, relationship. The idea that consumer-friendly techniques could be used to streamline data privacy protection and create public trust has been around since the 1990s. It was then that relevant initiatives first came into life, particularly in those parts of the world that chose not to enact national data protection legislation and preferred self-regulatory measures to provide 'visible' forms of privacy assurance to consumers as a means of gaining their trust. This trend did not pass unnoticed by hardline personal data protection proponents: EU Member States applying the 1995 EU Data Protection Directive 95/46/EC, that allegedly until today sets the global standard for a high level of data protection, also experimented with certification mechanisms in the data protection context within their respective jurisdictions. Admittedly, few of these early attempts are still alive today or have succeeded in their global aspirations. Outside the EU, negative media publicity did not assist the public image of privacy seals either.

Vagelis Papakonstantinou is Legal scholar in Brussels, Belgium, senior researcher at the Vrije Universiteit Brussel, practicing attorney in Athens, Greece, where he has co-founded and runs MPlegal, a law firm. Email: vagelis@papakonstantinou.me.

V. Papakonstantinou (✉)
Vrije Universiteit Brussel, Brussels, Belgium
e-mail: vagelis@papakonstantinou.me

© T.M.C. ASSER PRESS and the authors 2018
R. Rodrigues and V. Papakonstantinou (eds.), *Privacy and Data Protection Seals*,
Information Technology and Law Series 28, https://doi.org/10.1007/978-94-6265-228-6_1

However, perhaps unexpectedly, the past few years have witnessed a transformation of certification mechanisms from practically an outcast, to a central actor in the international data privacy arena. In Europe, while in the past attempts to implement seal programmes in EU Member States took off (e.g., France, Germany) or terminated mostly unobserved, the soon to come into effect EU General Data Protection Regulation (Regulation 2016/679) dedicates a whole section on this topic (Section 5, Chapter IV), treating certification mechanisms as an integral part of data controller and processor obligations. Outside Europe, privacy seal schemes that made it through the past decades have become more, or less institutionalised in their respective counties of origin, forming an integral part of their data privacy systems. Developments in the EU are bound to affect such schemes at a business, regulatory, and even conceptual level.

Some clarifications need to be made about this book to better approximate its aims and scope. First, on terminology: While some discussion among EU scholars exists as to whether the correct term is *"privacy seals"* or *"data protection seals"*, this book seeks to avoid this dilemma, because its scope is global and not just EU-centered. Therefore, while in the EU the General Data Protection Regulation refers to them as *"data protection seals"*, the fact remains that the term *"privacy seals"* has a broader dimension and is more widely internationally recognised—hence we use both the terms in the title of this book. Many a times, the distinction between the two terms is highly blurred. Similarly, for the purposes of this book, the terms "data protection" and "data privacy", unless expressly clarified otherwise in the relevant chapter, may be used as synonyms, interchangeably. For the unfamiliar reader, a privacy (or data protection) seal refers to any mark, symbol, icon, logo, stamp, or a guarantee that provides an assurance that a product or service or system complies with certain specified privacy (or data protection) standards or requirements.

Various entities play a part in privacy and data protection seals e.g., certifying authority or seal issuer (this might be a private company or a data protection authority), accreditation body, applicants, and the parties relying on privacy and/or data protection seals. In different contexts and domains these entities might be termed differently, e.g., as evident in the terminology used in the data protection versus consumer protection domains. In the data protection domain, the actors involved in the certification process might be termed differently to that in a consumer protection domain. Therefore, a strict uniform categorisation of the parties involved in the privacy seal process is not imposed in this book; this is left open for exploration in the individual chapters. In addition, the privacy seals field is yet unsettled and since the Article 29 Working Party is working guidance on certification, we considered it best not to intervene in this process, but rather to highlight the relevant difficulty, so as for it to be taken into consideration in the future.

Another necessary clarification pertains to the concept of *"seals"*. This book adopts a broad approach to cover any, and all cases of privacy seals—online or offline. Consequently, a seal may be electronic, essentially aimed at being affixed on a website, or *"physical"* in the sense that it may manifest offline, placed, for instance, on a product. Similarly, we do not dwell on the distinction between goods and services. Privacy and/or data protection seals are applicable in both contexts. A seal may certify that a certain product (e.g., video management software) meets a set privacy standard and requirements; in the same way, a seal could certify a certain service (e.g., online matchmaking service). A seal may also certify that a manufacturing process or the provision of a service process adheres to certain privacy standards.

This book brings together much needed and timely contributions on privacy and data protection seals from experts in the field. It covers the following topics: certification and seals in the EU General Data Protection Regulation; national data protection authority privacy seal schemes (France and Germany); privacy seals in USA, Europe, Japan, Canada, India and Australia; controversies and challenges; privacy seals and their potential for deployment in emerging technologies; and economics of privacy seals. As of writing there is, to the editors' knowledge at least, no other book bringing together privacy and data protection seals. While some books have focused on trustmarks and web assurance seals and several articles have been published between 2005 and 2017 on privacy seals, none of these publications offer the kind of analysis this book proposes, or mirrors its unique arrangement. This book will appeal to European legislators, policymakers, privacy and data protection practitioners, certification bodies, international organisations, and academics. This book is particularly relevant and significant in the EU context, given the recognition in the proposed General Data Protection Regulation to certification mechanisms, seals and marks as a means of allowing data subjects to quickly, reliably and verifiably assess the level of data protection of relevant products and services and the increasing policy attention being given to privacy and data protection seals.

The aims of the book broadly are: to provide a much needed overview of privacy and data protection seals; to compare privacy, data protection certification schemes; to discuss EU policy and legislative developments on privacy and data protection seals particularly the provisions of the EU General Data Protection Regulation (which awards to seals, along with other certification mechanisms, a central place with regard to data controller and processor obligations); to analyse privacy, data protection certification schemes run by data protection authorities (to enable gain insight into their practical implementation); and to understand the challenges, economics and future (technological) applicability of privacy seals. The analyses in the book are aimed to be practical too, in the sense that specific case studies, in the form of seals' programmes already in operation are elaborated in the chapters that follow. This was considered necessary to demonstrate the contemporary state of the art and to help extract useful lessons for similar future implementations.

The editors' interest in and involvement with the privacy seals field dates back to 2012. We understand that this interest may seem relatively late, given that discussions on the usefulness of such a system for the data protection purposes may be traced, mostly in German legal theory, as early as the nineties. However, the intermediate period, that spans until today, could probably be characterised as a testing, pilot phase. In practice, our research demonstrated that, until 2014 at least, the privacy seal schemes in operation in the EU were heterogeneous in nature, underpinned by different types of criteria and requirements, and plagued, among others, by a pick-and-mix regulatory approach, vagueness, lack of support for data subject rights and lack of clarity about their scope. Some schemes were not easily accessible or robust enough (some schemes had dubious credentials and missing information). In essence, we established that the lack of any formal regulatory guidance meant that each privacy certifiers/seal issuers in the field adopted their own model, under their own assumptions, terms and specifications, which served different purposes. All this is not clear to persons relying on privacy seals as a means of gaining positive assurances about the protection of their privacy or protection of their personal data. Seals schemes varied from formal programmes introduced and run by data protection authorities, to for-profit initiatives run by consultancies. Outside the EU, the variety of legal statuses granted to seal schemes essentially meant that a detailed comparative law analysis was necessary if any meaningful conclusions about their effectiveness for the protection of individual privacy were to be drawn.

Given this scenario, we felt that a great opportunity was wasted. Seals, and other certification mechanisms, have a lot to offer both for privacy and data protection. From the data subject perspective, they offer the means to quickly ascertain the adequacy of data protection in an increasingly complex online and offline world where fast-moving technological developments mean their privacy and personal data are at constant risk from myriad threats. For data controllers, where used correctly, privacy seals may offer legal certainty and, hopefully, a competitive advantage in the market. Data protection authorities could profit from all the help they could get while assessing compliance in market conditions where constantly a larger number of parties is engaging at a rapid rate in different forms of data processing. Accreditation bodies could benefit from the opening of an aspiring new market to certify 'good' privacy seal schemes and fields of related activities. If the data protection certification model specified in the GDPR takes off, the EU itself could benefit not only indirectly, through the commercial competitive advantage for EU enterprises in a globalised, hyperconnected world, but also directly from the development of a demonstrably functional, and thus exportable, tool for data privacy management.

Despite of the fact that the potential benefits of certification span several market sectors and fields of law, the perspective in this book is decidedly privacy-related. Although a lot can be said about seals, for example, about their social or market function, or if viewed from a standards and competition law point of view, this book adopts a mostly data privacy viewpoint. In the same context, individuals are here treated as *data subjects* and not exclusively as consumers—a different role that would lead to a different perspective on this matter. Seals' users, from their part, are treated as *controllers* and not just as sellers of products or service providers. Maybe research that would combine all these roles, in the form of a follow-up to this book, would be helpful in the future, as an effort to further elucidate the potential function of seals' schemes in the data privacy field.

In Chap. 2, Irene Kamara and Paul de Hert discuss the EU General Data Protection Regulation approach to certification in the data protection field. They briefly go over the law-making process of the Regulation, before looking at the five building blocks of the certification system developed in Articles 42 and 43 of the Regulation: data protection certification mechanisms, accreditation, oversight, role of the European Data Protection Board and the role of the European Commission. They argue that the GDPR data protection certification mechanisms are overall a positive step of the EU regulator towards embracing soft law instruments as a means to demonstrate compliance with the GDPR.

Next, the book tackles two short, case study examples of privacy seal schemes run by national data protection authorities. Chapter 3 by Marit Hansen discusses the Schleswig-Holstein Data Protection Seal ("Datenschutz-Gütesiegel Schleswig-Holstein"), a programme running for more than fifteen years that is addressed predominantly to the German market. Apart from presenting its legal and operational background, the author lists the lessons learnt from this long process, an indispensable guidance for future national or EU implementations of data protection seals.

France is until today the only EU Member State that has implemented a formal, data protection authority-driven, nation-wide privacy seals programme as early as in 2011. Evidently, countries both within and outside the EU have a lot to learn from what CNIL itself still characterises as an experiment in its early stages. In Chap. 4, Johanna Carvais-Palut presents the unique approach applied by CNIL, namely that, instead of "issuing a seal certifying compliance with the law", CNIL "chose to deliver seals to organisations whose products and procedures are exemplary; a seal that rewards those most deserving and principled, giving them recognition and distinction for going above and beyond what the law requires".

It is, however, outside EU boundaries that data privacy certification gained wider public use over the past decades. In Chap. 5, Ann Cavoukian and Michelle Chibba present a comparative analysis of privacy seals in the USA, Japan, Canada India and Australia. Their focus is particularly on schemes that have a history of more than ten years. This filter brought under their radar two European trustmarks, among which is EuroPriSe, a spin-off of the Schleswig-Holstein Data Protection Seal. The authors conclude that privacy seals could come into their own as a powerful facilitator of globalisation of consumer transactions, if they are able to provide acceptable and enforceable privacy protection across multiple jurisdictions.

In Chap. 6, Paolo Balboni and Theodora Dragan discuss controversies and challenges related to data protection seals. They first focus on the role of trustmarks in e-commerce, to draw lessons learnt that may prove useful while implementing seals programmes in the data privacy field. Subsequently, they adopt a practical perspective, whereby they carry out useful empirical research into the practices of several EU-based trustmark providers to identify shortcomings and key factors of seal programmes success. Trustmarks need to reach critical mass and to stimulate awareness. The authors make concrete recommendations, addressed both at regulators and stakeholders.

Challenges to privacy seals, however, not only originate from the regulatory framework in effect. Emerging technologies continuously test their scope and relevance to the data protection purposes. Chapter 7 by David Barnard-Wills explores the relationship between privacy seals and emerging technologies using case-specific examples of the Internet of Things (IoT), smart homes, smart cars, wearables and drones from a theoretical privacy seals perspective. The author derives from these thought experiments the requirement for any effective privacy seals programme, i.e., a strong alignment between the technology and its social context of use.

In Chap. 8, Patrick Waelbroeck provides an economic analysis of privacy seals. Privacy seals are essentially a market tool that needs to remain sustainable. The author focuses on three aspects in this regard: the demand for, and supply of privacy protection, the economic trade-offs and the business model of a typical privacy seals programme, and its possible economic impacts. The relevant discussion is extremely interesting, relevant, and yet unresolved, evidenced in a list of open questions that remain to be answered by stakeholders and regulators alike.

Without wishing to prejudice the readers' approach on the topics above, or the concluding remarks (Chap. 9) prepared by my co-editor, Rowena Rodrigues, if a common base line among the chapters that follow was to be established, I believe that it would refer to the common finding that privacy seals are indeed useful tools that have a lot to offer for data protection purposes. This coincides with our research findings dating back to 2014, and with our initial perception on this matter while planning this book with the kind assistance of Dr. Eleni Kosta, series co-editor of the Springer Information Technology and Law Series, and Frank Bakker from our generous publisher, T.M.C. Asser Press, something that is itself a lucky outcome for any researcher. We hope that our book will offer some useful insights into the global discussion on privacy and data protection seals, at a time when the value of it is in both in question and has simultaneously become greatly enhanced by EU data protection law.

Chapter 2
Data Protection Certification in the EU: Possibilities, Actors and Building Blocks in a Reformed Landscape

Irene Kamara and Paul De Hert

Contents

Irene Kamara, Tilburg University (TILT), Vrije Universiteit Brussel (LSTS) irene.kamara@vub.be; Prof. Paul De Hert, Vrije Universiteit Brussel (LSTS), Tilburg University (TILT) paul.de.hert@vub.be.

I. Kamara (✉) · P. De Hert
Tilburg University (TILT), Tilburg, The Netherlands
e-mail: irene.kamara@vub.be

P. De Hert
e-mail: paul.de.hert@vub.be

I. Kamara · P. De Hert
Vrije Universiteit Brussel (LSTS), Brussel, Belgium

© T.M.C. ASSER PRESS and the authors 2018
R. Rodrigues and V. Papakonstantinou (eds.), *Privacy and Data Protection Seals*,
Information Technology and Law Series 28, https://doi.org/10.1007/978-94-6265-228-6_2

Abstract Certification and seals as a form of co-regulation have been on the EU agenda for over a decade. Enhancing consumer trust and promoting transparency and compliance are central arguments in the policy endorsement for certification. In the field of data protection, the General Data Protection Regulation has substantiated considerably these policy objectives of the European Commission. Our contribution discusses the new legal EU regime for data protection certification. Starting from the background of data protection certification and the preparatory works of the General Data Protection Regulation, the chapter analyses the legal provisions in the new EU data protection framework and reflects on the steps after the Regulation starts to apply.

Keywords Certification · seals · marks · privacy · personal data protection · General Data Protection Regulation

2.1 Background and Structure of the Contribution

Certification, seals and (trust)marks have long been used in commerce and digital transactions to enhance transparency, facilitate consumer choice and urge providers to comply with legislation.[1] Certification comes in all forms and sectors, by diverse stakeholders and is highly unregulated by legal instruments. These features explain why certification is controversial and often contested as not delivering promised safeguards to the consumer.[2] The criticism mainly targets certifications that are disconnected from regulatory oversight and may have deceptive potential.[3] However, we believe it is possible to guarantee both transparency and effective enforcement.

---

[1] Certification, seals and marks are interrelated. Certification is related to the certification process which includes assessment against pre-defined requirements. The successful process leads to the issue of a certificate. Both seals and marks are visualisations of statements of conformity of a product, process or service with the pre-defined requirements. A mark (of conformity) is the indication that an object is in conformity with specified requirements based on a successful certification procedure. The seal is a visual representation of the successful process, usually including a unique number for each entity that is entitled to use the seal, and in contrast to the mark, can be legally binding per se.

[2] Greenleaf for instance argues that "there is very little evidence, from what we have seen in the last forty years, that any non-legal constraints will prove effective against business and government self-interest in expanded surveillance: this applies to voluntary self-regulation (through codes of conduct, standard-setting, privacy seals, or spontaneous adoption of privacy-enhancing technologies (PETs) or privacy-by design), the force of competition, or the adoption by consumers of PETs and counter-surveillance technologies." Greenleaf 2012.

[3] For instance, in November 2014, the Federal Trade Commission (FTC) settled with the online privacy seal provider TRUSTe on a complaint about TRUSTe failing to conduct promised annual re-certifications of companies participating in its privacy seal program more than 1,000 times between 2006 and 2013. The complaint also alleged that TRUSTe misrepresented its status as a non-profit entity. See Federal Trade Commission 2015.

The Directive 95/46/EC[4] did not include any requirements on certification or seals in relation to data protection. A reference to self-regulation was made in Article 27 of the Directive, which encouraged the use of codes of conduct at the national and European level. The lack of an explicit provision on data protection certification has not hindered activity in the field. Various privacy seals and schemes were developed based on the Directive requirements for data controllers and processors. A prominent example is the EuroPriSe seal, developed by an EU-funded research project. The EuroPriSe seal criteria are based on the Directive 95/46/EC, the ePrivacy Directive[5] and other relevant EU legislation.[6] At national level, there are several seals operated and granted by the data protection authorities (based on national legislation implementing the Data Protection Directive) and private bodies. This activity shows that the lack of legal basis in the EU data protection framework did not hold back initiatives developing data protection seals and schemes. On the other hand, the number of certified entities is not particularly high,[7] which shows that controllers are hesitant to undergo an often, costly process if the certification does not have an added value for their business. The multitude of such seals, and a general sense of lack of public trust and confidence in those schemes have been identified as gaps of existing schemes.[8] Such factors have contributed to the direction of official regulatory endorsement and the inclusion of certification in the new data protection framework in the EU.

The European Commission included trustmarks in its policy objectives in the *Digital Agenda for Europe* in 2010 as means to enhance user trust regarding the security of payments and privacy.[9] In addition, the *Cybersecurity Strategy* prioritised EU-wide voluntary certification in cloud computing and invited stakeholders to "develop industry-led standards for companies' performance on cybersecurity and improve the information available to the public by developing security labels or kite marks helping the consumer navigate the market."[10] The European Data Protection Supervisor (EDPS) has also upheld privacy seals with third-party audit as a means for an organisation to demonstrate its interest in privacy and data

---

[4] European Parliament and Council, Directive 95/46/EC of the European Parliament and of the Council of 24 October 1995 on the protection of individuals with regard to the processing of personal data and on the free movement of such data (Data Protection Directive) OJ L 281, 23.11.1995.

[5] European Parliament and the Council, Directive 2002/58/EC.

[6] EuroPriSe criteria, November 2011, https://www.european-privacy-seal.eu/EPS-en/Criteria. Accessed 10 January 2017.

[7] For instance EuroPriSe awarded eleven seals in 2015, six of which were re-certification. https://www.european-privacy-seal.eu/EPS-en/Awarded-seals. Accessed 10 January 2017.

[8] De Hert et al. 2014, p. 11f.

[9] European Commission 2010.

[10] European Commission 2013, Cybersecurity strategy.

protection.[11] Since 2010, there have been studies recommending a 'careful' endorsement of data protection certification mechanisms in EU legislation.[12] Finally, the General Data Protection Regulation (GDPR) on the protection of individuals with regard to the processing of personal data and on the free movement of such data formally endorses data protection certification in Articles 42 and 43.

Sections 2.2–2.4 of this chapter discuss briefly the travaux préparatoires of Articles 42 and 43 (formerly 39 and 39a in previous versions) of the General Data Protection Regulation. The European Commission proposal,[13] European Parliament first reading[14] and the Council first reading[15] all included provisions on certification, seals and marks. The vision of each body however differed significantly in terms of organisation of the certification mechanism, binding effect, regulatory oversight, and legal consequences. The European Commission proposed a framework of encouragement and acknowledgement of the importance of data protection certification; the European Parliament envisaged a European Data Protection Seal managed by the data protection authorities and the European Data Protection Board, while the Council proposed a more flexible model and allocated the certification process to accredited private bodies, without excluding data protection authorities. Sections 2.2–2.4 outline the main points of the three different approaches of the GDPR towards certification to better understand the final text of the Regulation.

The final text of the Regulation on certification is looked at in Sects. 2.5–2.10. We analyse in detail the five building blocks of the certification system developed in Articles 42 and 43 GDPR: data protection certification mechanism, accreditation, oversight, role of the European Data Protection Board and role of the European Commission. Data protection certification mechanisms are not a mandatory measure for data controllers or processors, but an optional decision. Section 2.11 discusses the certification effects and the voluntary nature of data protection certification. Section 2.12 outlines the foreseen use, added value and benefits of the Articles 42 and 43 certification mechanism in five cases. Section 2.13 concludes the chapter with reflection on the new system and the next steps for its implementation. We argue that the GDPR data protection certification mechanisms are, overall, a positive step of the EU regulator towards embracing soft law instruments as a means to demonstrate compliance with the GDPR. The successful implementation of the mechanisms will depend on maintaining a balance between endorsing and facilitating the GDPR certification, and at the same time guaranteeing that all necessary safeguards are in place to protect the right to personal data protection.

---

[11] Hustinx 2008, p. 561.
[12] EC DG Justice 2010, p. 53f.
[13] EC Proposal (2012) Proposal for a Regulation.
[14] European Parliament (2014) First Reading.
[15] European Council (2015) First Reading.

2.2 The 2012 Commission Proposal: Endorsement of Certification Mechanisms and Seals

In 2009, the Commission launched a review of the legal framework on data protection. A high-level conference in May 2009, a public consultation and several studies, highlighted that the core principles of the Directive 95/46/EC were still valid. At the same time, several issues were identified as problematic[16] and thus called for the development of a new framework to protect the right to protection of personal data. The Commission prioritised key actions to respond to the identified challenges. Among those key actions was the enhancement of the internal market dimension through the encouragement of self-regulatory initiatives and EU certification schemes. EU certification schemes (e.g. privacy seals) for 'privacy-compliant' processes, technologies, products and services, were envisaged as having a double function in terms of both *transparency of processing* and *controller responsibility*. The schemes would 'give an orientation' to the individual user of such technologies, products and services and in parallel they would be relevant for data controllers, to *help to prove* that a controller has fulfilled his or her obligations. The Commission also stressed the importance of trustworthiness of the privacy seals.

The 2012 European Commission Regulation proposal introduced a new provision on data protection certification.[17] Article 39 of the Commission Proposal, introduced under Section 5 "Codes of Conduct and Certification", highlighted the instrumental role certification and marks can play in the promotion of compliance with the GDPR. The EC proposal handled data protection certification mechanisms, the data protection seals and marks as an instrument to enhance transparency and compliance with the Regulation. The establishment of such mechanisms and seals would allow "data subjects to quickly assess the level of data protection of relevant products and services". Transparency was a prominent element of the proposed provision, aiming to facilitate the assessment of the level of protection offered by the product or the service. The proposal of the Commission did not specify the issuing body of the certificates, nor the procedure of the certification. A reserved role for the Commission was the one of the adoption of *delegated acts* for specifying the criteria and requirements for data protection mechanisms. The proposal of the Commission was undoubtedly a positive step towards the recognition of data protection certification, seals and marks. This step can be seen as a positive

---

[16] The problematic areas were the following: 1. The impact of new technologies 2. The enhancement of the internal market dimension of data protection 3. Addressing the globalisation and improvement of international data transfers 4. The effective enforcement of data protection rules and 5. The coherence of data protection legal framework. See COM (2010) 609 final.

[17] European Commission 2012, Proposal for a Regulation of the European Parliament and of the Council on the protection of individuals with regard to the processing of personal data and on the free movement of such data (General Data Protection Regulation) COM (2012) 11 final—2012/0011 (COD), 25.01.2012.

embracement of certification in the field of personal data protection, while abstaining from regulating in more detail important issues such as the regulatory overview and the enforcement. The flexibility of the EC proposal in terms of function and aim of data protection certification, in combination with the lack of definitions of "seals", "marks" and "certification", left room for broad interpretation of what was accepted and what was not "data protection certification" according to the proposal. The risk of such an elastic approach is the weakening of the concept of the data protection certification itself. A market overcrowded with certified products and seals that offer no assurance for actual protection would risk rather than facilitate the protection of the data subjects' rights.

2.3   The 2014 European Parliament First Reading: The European Data Protection Seal

The European Parliament in its first reading in 2014 went one step further in regulating data protection certification mechanisms by introducing a new concept, the "European Data Protection Seal" i.e., a harmonised data protection seal at EU level.[18] Article 39 of the Parliament version of the Regulation stipulated that the certification and seal would be issued and awarded by the supervisory authorities. To ensure harmonised results, the consistency mechanism of Article 57 of the Regulation would apply. The supervisory authorities would have the power to accredit *specialised third party auditors* to carry out the auditing of the controller or the processor *on their behalf.* Acting as agents on behalf of the supervisory authorities, the auditors would have to follow strictly the instructions of the data protection authorities, with a risk of liability in the opposite case. The Commission would have the power to adopt delegated acts in line with Article 86 to further specify the criteria and requirements for the data protection certification mechanisms, including requirements for accreditation of auditors, conditions for granting and withdrawal, and requirements for recognition within the Union and in third countries, as in the EC proposal. The only obligation of the Commission would be a *request* for an opinion of the European Data Protection Board and consultation with stakeholders, in a specific industry and non-governmental organisations, prior to the adoption of the acts. The result of the opinion and consultation would not be binding for the European Commission. This means that in case the European Data Protection Board would have issued a negative opinion, the Commission could still proceed with adopting the act. The provision for consultation with stakeholders would essentially work towards ensuring that the criteria and requirements were not

---

[18] European   Parliament   2014   (http://www.europarl.europa.eu/sides/getDoc.do?type=TA&language=EN&reference=P7-TA-2014-0212). Accessed 10 June 2016.

disconnected from the market needs and data subject's concerns.[19] As Korff notes, the actual issuing of a seal by a data protection authority would constitute an administrative act of such an authority (Article 53(1)(ia))[20] with legally binding effects. The granting of the seal would mean compliance with the GDPR. As a general assessment, the proposal of the Parliament intended to develop a strong EU recognisable data protection certification mechanism and seal.

2.4   The 2015 Council First Reading: Data Protection Seals as an Element of Accountability

The Council did not follow the European Parliament's view on a European Data Protection Seal, but rather promoted a certification model using the existing certification market, i.e. certification bodies. The Council treated data protection certification as an element of accountability for data controllers and processors, without legally binding results for the supervisory authorities. In the text of the Council, there was a new addition, Article 39a, which described the accreditation of the certification body.

The proposed amendments by the Council regarding Article 39 received criticism,[21] as lacking the necessary regulatory assurances and oversight.[22] The main issue with this proposal was that the decision to grant the certification was made by the accredited private certification body, instead of the supervisory authority.

We will see in the following section that the Council's proposals regarding Articles 39 and 39a became an almost final blueprint for the final text of the GDPR.[23]

---

[19] Even though such consultation in practice would probably offer a wide range of opposing opinions, challenging to reconcile, if a "positive approval" or "endorsement" would be required.

[20] Korff 2014.

[21] Douwe Korff argues that: "(..) *the Council would allow Member States to either opt for relatively strong seals issued by DPAs (such as the French Labels), or for an almost completely out-sourced certification scheme under which seals would be issued by an accredited certification body separate from the DPA (and not subject to directions from the DPA, other than in terms of general guidance). The out-sourced seals would have no formal legal effect—but would also by-pass all European cooperation and consistency mechanisms. Yet they would still in practice largely exempt the companies that were awarded such seals from enforcement action by the DPA in question (as long as they complied with the conditions etc. set out in the seals).*" in Korff 2014, para 3.

[22] EDRi and Privacy International on a common statement published in June 2015 under the title "Privacy and Data Protection under threat from EU Council agreement" said that the Council version opens the gates to a "massive Trojan Horse" in particularly with regard to the articles that refer to certification mechanisms and data transfers, Järvinen 2015.

[23] In the final text of the GDPR the numbering of the certification articles changed from 39 and 39a (in the European Commission Proposal, the first reading of the Parliament and the Council) to 42 and 43.

2.5   Articles 42 and 43 GDPR on Data Protection Certification

In December 2015, a political deal was struck on the EU Data Protection Reform of 2012.[24] In May 2016, the GDPR was published in the Official Journal of the EU.[25] The provisions for the data protection certification mechanism are included in Articles 42 and 43 of the GDPR, complemented mainly by Articles 57, 58, 64, 70 and 83. Several other provisions and recitals in the Regulation refer to certification as a measure. The GDPR establishes a rather complex certification mechanism which involves the existing certification landscape adapted to the needs of the protection of a fundamental right. The new certification mechanism calls for an active role by national supervisory authorities, the European Data Protection Board and the European Commission. The mechanism seems to be an attempt to satisfy both market and industry needs for certification schemes, seals and marks, and address self-regulation sceptics and the demands for regulatory oversight. The tensions are apparent throughout the text of the GDPR and the end-result of the new system strikes a fragile balance between these opposing tensions.

Articles 42 and 43 are the cornerstones of the new certification mechanism.[26] They introduce the aim of data protection certification in the framework of the GDPR and provide general requirements regarding the certification bodies and the organisation of the data protection certification mechanism. The data protection certification mechanism of the GDPR is third-party certification. In distinction from self-regulation initiatives, such as Privacy Shield which is a system of self-declaration of conformance to the requirements of the Privacy Shield framework, the certification mechanism under Articles 42 and 43 is audited by third party independent certification bodies and supervised by data protection authorities. The data protection mechanism envisaged by the European regulator in Article 42 involves mainly two actors: certification bodies[27] and supervisory authorities, namely the data protection authorities (i.e., Information Commissioners) of the EU Member States.

---

[24] The agreement was on the General Data Protection Regulation and the Data protection directive in law enforcement intended to replace the Council Framework Decision 2008/977/JHA of 27 November 2008 on the protection of personal data processed in the framework of police and judicial cooperation in criminal matters.

[25] European Parliament and Council of the European Union 2016.

[26] Before going into detailed analysis of the provisions, note that what is envisaged in the Regulation are two different certifications: the national certification based on the GDPR and the 'common certification', the European Data Protection Seal. Most of the provisions are dedicated to the national certification mechanism, which is therefore the focus of this contribution. The provision for the European Data Protection Seal is briefly discussed.

[27] A certification body is a "third-party conformity assessment body, which operates certification schemes" ISO/IEC 17065:2012, Conformity assessment—Requirements for bodies certifying products, processes and services.

The GDPR provides a data protection certification mechanism built on the current certification practice as it entails certification with the involvement of a certification body.[28] At the same time, it reserves a substantial role for the supervisory authorities at several stages of the certification procedure.[29] The emphasis upon oversight and control, also evident in the organisation of the mechanism and the accreditation process, can be said to characterise the EU view on data protection certification.

In the following sections, we identify the five building blocks of the certification system developed in Articles 42 and 43 of the GDPR.

2.6   The Certification Process in the General Data Protection Regulation (Building Block 1)

Before explaining in detail the certification process in the GDPR, it should be underlined that the text of the GDPR does not define the terms 'certification', 'seals' and 'marks'. There is also a gap in determining any differences in the granting, use, and revocation between certifications, seals and marks, and the relationship of the three instruments. As the terms in current certification practice are not used in a uniform way, the lack of clarity in the text of the GDPR might lead to uncertainty as to the characteristics, role, and legal significance of each of them, and compromise a harmonised implementation of the data protection certification mechanisms.[30]

Regarding the certification process, the role of a certification body is to assess the conformity of the product, process or service with pre-defined requirements ('conformity assessment') and provide a certificate of conformity. Usually those requirements are included either in a technical standard or the law.[31] The requirements for the assessment process, the certification body, the competencies of the personnel involved (e.g. auditors), the certificate (e.g. the period of validity) and the conditions for granting the certificate or the mark or seal are included in the *certification scheme*, a document developed, owned and operated by organisations such as certification bodies, industry associations, public authorities or other (e.g. the scheme owner). The range of potential scheme owners is broad and depends on the aims of the certification, the type of product or system and its application area. Since there is no harmonised cross-sectorial legislation on certification at the European level, the certification market is governed by a private system of technical standards that set rules and requirements for certification.

---

[28] Article 42 GDPR.

[29] See Article 58 GDPR, investigative, corrective, and authorisation powers of the supervisory authorities in relation to data protection certification mechanisms.

[30] ENISA 2017.

[31] See Sect. 2.10 for a discussion on the criteria.

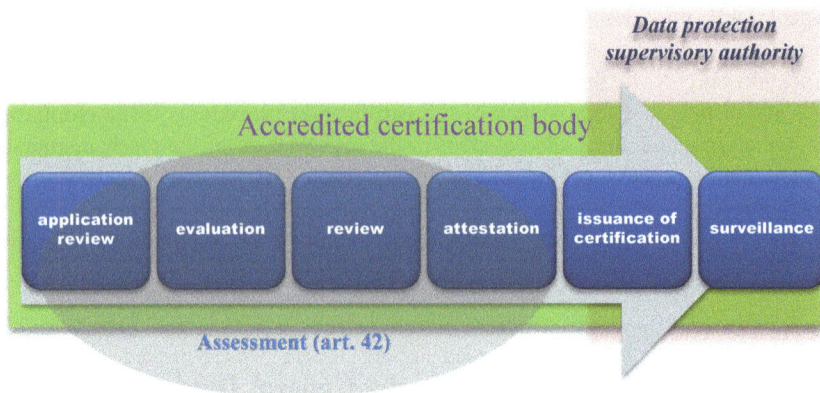

Fig. 2.1 ISO/IEC 17065 stages of certification process adapted to the Article 42 GDPR mechanism [Source: I. Kamara and P. De Hert]

In current certification practice, the international standard ISO/IEC 17065 (Fig. 2.1), which is also adopted as a European Standard (EN), is widely used.[32] The process according to the standard, as presented in Graphic 1, starts with an application by the interested party to the certification body. The certification body reviews the application by checking the provision of information in the application, the scope of the application, whether the applicant is competent and has the capacity for the requested certification. An acceptance to undertake the certification takes the procedure to the following stage of evaluation of the certification application. The evaluation is performed with resources of the certification body or outsourced resources, usually when there is a need for testing in laboratories or similar activities. The evaluation is performed against pre-defined requirements. When for instance an organisation applies for certification of its quality management against ISO 9001:2015 standard, the assessment process evaluates the system against the requirements included in the ISO 9001:2015 standard. The evaluation results show to what extent the product, process, or service under evaluation conforms to the requirements. If the evaluation results are satisfactory, a reviewer or more—other than persons involved in the evaluation phase—review the results. Following this phase, the certification body makes the decision on whether to grant the certification. Experts who participated in the evaluation phase are excluded from the decision stage. In many certification schemes, there is also the stage of post-certification monitoring ("surveillance") that the certified product, system or service continues to fulfil the requirements after the issuance of the certificate. This stage is particularly important for enhancing the transparency and trust from the part of consumers to the certification process.

---

[32] Although the certification field is not harmonised at EU level, the certification phases of the EN-ISO/IEC 17065 standard are most commonly followed in practice.

The data protection certification mechanism enshrined in Articles 42 and 43 of GDPR is inspired by the stages of the international ISO/IEC 17065 (Fig. 2.1).[33] In principle, the certification body performs most of the stages of the data protection certification procedure. The certification body is responsible for the proper assessment leading to certification (Articles 42(6), 43(4)), issues (Articles 42(5), 43 (1)) and renews the certificates (Articles 42(7), 43(1)), after informing the supervisory authority. When the requirements for the data protection certification are no longer met, the certification body is obliged to withdraw the certification.

The GDPR however also provides that the supervisory authority may issue[34] and withdraw the certification.[35] Moreover, the supervisory authority may order the certification body not to renew a data protection certification. The interpretation of the letter of the Regulation is not particularly informative as to *when* the supervisory authority has those powers instead of the certification body. The Regulation uses expressions such as "where applicable" to indicate where such power is given to the supervisory authority, without however further specifying the conditions.[36] The relevant Articles 57 and 58 GDPR do not provide further conditions, which leads to the conclusion that the Regulator intentionally allowed for flexibility to the Member States in that respect. In practice, there will have to be rules at the national level on that issue, to ensure a uniform relationship between the competent supervisory authority and each accredited certification body. To ensure uniform application of the GDPR regarding Articles 42 and 43, the rules at national level would need to be agreed first at European level, most likely via the European Data Protection Board or the European Commission with implementing acts (Article 43 (9)). This would also help avoid unwanted competition with data protection mechanisms that are operated by supervisory authorities.[37]

---

[33] This is a rather important novelty of the GDPR because the regulator endorses a technical standard that was developed at international level. Article 43(1)(b) also makes an explicit reference to the ISO/IEC standard. It should be noted that the reference to the standard is *static*, meaning that the GDPR refers only to the specific version of the ISO/IEC: 17065 of 2012, and not to any future updates. This can be considered as a safer choice for the GDPR, as the regulator refers to the specific *known* content of the standard, even though the static reference of standards in the legislation always entails the risk to render the reference obsolete, once the standard is revised or updated.

[34] Among their authorisation and advisory powers, the supervisory authorities have the power to issue certifications (Article 58(3)(f)).

[35] Among their corrective powers, the supervisory authorities have the power to withdraw a certification or order to the certification body to withdraw or not to issue a certification (Article 58 (2)(h)).

[36] The issue of both accredited certification bodies and the supervisory authorities having the power to grant certificates is also highlighted by the Bavarian Data Protection Authority for the Private Sector (2016).

[37] See Rodrigues et al. 2016, p. 19.

2.7 Accredited Certification Bodies: "Certifying the Certifiers" (Building Block 2)

The diversity of the certification landscape creates a need to assure the quality and independence of certification activities and build trust in the private mechanisms of conformity assessment bodies.[38] Such impartial and objective oversight is provided through *accreditation*. Accreditation "provides an authoritative statement of the technical competence of bodies whose task is to assure conformity with the applicable requirements".[39] The matter is thoroughly addressed in EU law: Regulation 765/2008[40] organises the accreditation of certification and conformity assessment bodies (laboratories, inspection bodies, etc.) and obliges Member States to establish a National Accreditation Body to exercise public authority into evaluating whether a conformity assessment body is competent to carry out a specific conformity assessment activity.[41] The National Accreditation Bodies issue accreditation certificates once the evaluation of the conformity assessment body is successful. Another obligation of each National Accreditation Body is to monitor the conformance of the accredited body.

The GDPR acknowledges the existence of an accreditation system at the EU level by explicitly referring to the above Regulation on accreditation in Article 43 (1)(b). However, the accreditation system under the GDPR does not necessarily involve the National Accreditation Body in each case as described above, but leaves the choice to the Member States to provide whether the certification bodies involved in the data protection certification mechanisms are accredited by the (data protection) supervisory authority only (Article 43(1)(a)), by the National Accreditation Body *with the additional requirements established by* the supervisory authority (Article 43(1)(b)), or by both. In the case of combining both accreditation means, the GDPR uses the existing experience of National Accreditation Bodies and requires the involvement of the supervisory authority with regard to 'additional requirements', assumingly referring to specific capacity requirements related to data protection. The GDPR provides different options therefore for the accreditation of certification bodies and the Member States may choose that certification bodies are accredited either by one of those options *or by both* (Article 43(1)).

However, accreditation of certification bodies by the supervisory authority alone (Article 43(1)(a)) could prove to be problematic in several aspects. First, not all the data protection authorities[42] have experience in certification and seals and even less

---

[38] Conformity assessment body is a "body that performs conformity assessment activities including calibration, testing, certification and inspection", Regulation 765/2008 of the Article 2 (13).

[39] Regulation (EC) 765/2008 Recital 9.

[40] Regulation (EC) 765/2008.

[41] Regulation 765/2008 Article 5(1).

[42] The terms supervisory authorities and Data Protection Authorities are used interchangeably in this chapter.

in accreditation. Although data protection authorities will need to familiarise their personnel with such processes in line with their new tasks and powers, there is a substantial lack of experience in this field for most of the supervisory authorities in comparison to the National Accreditation Bodies. In addition, supervisory authorities are particularly empowered in the GDPR with several tasks and powers (Articles 57 and 58), but their limited resources remain a significant issue.[43] Moreover and most importantly, the scope of accreditation should not be limited to the data protection requirements, but extend to management, process, resources, legal, liability, confidentiality and other requirements.[44] A certification body should fulfil all the above requirements. Otherwise, a certification body accredited by a supervisory authority, that for instance does not fulfil confidentiality and non-discriminatory requirements, would not offer reliable certification, despite the soundness of the data protection requirements. Even if the above issues were to be overcome, the very option of *choice* of the Member States between the options (only supervisory authorities *or* National Accreditation bodies with data protection requirements set by the supervisory authorities *or* both) would lead to non-harmonised application at EU level. In practice, it would be easier and more trustworthy to follow the option that involves both supervisory authorities and the National Accreditation Bodies. A supervisory authority could ask the certification body to be accredited by the (territorially) competent National Accreditation Body, before the supervisory authority proceeds to accredit the certification body in terms of personal data protection capacity.

To mitigate potential problems from the diverse implementation of the above accreditation system, Article 43(2) identifies a list of general requirements to provide minimum guarantees related to non-data protection accreditation requirements. Article 43(2) provides the certification body needs to have demonstrated its independence and expertise in relation to the subject-matter of certification "to the satisfaction of the competent supervisory authority", to have established procedures for issuing, periodic review and withdrawal of certification, seals and marks and to have established transparent complaint mechanisms. These requirements are inspired by the EN-ISO/IEC 17065:2012 standard on requirements for bodies certifying products, processes, and services.[45] Additionally, there are requirements

---

[43] A survey conducted by the EU-funded PHAEDRA project found that most data protection authorities in the EU Member States have fewer than 60 staff. Wright et al. 2015, p. 20.

[44] ISO/IEC 17065:2012, Conformity assessment—Requirements for bodies certifying products, processes and services.

[45] The ISO/IEC 17065:2012 includes similar provisions with the Article 43(2) GDPR. For instance, there are process requirements (section 7, pp.), complaints handling (section 7.13, p. 19), requirements related to impartiality of the certification body (management of impartiality in section 4.2 and mechanism for safeguarding impartiality in section 5.2), requirement for publicly available information including information on procedures for handling complaints and appeals (section 4.6), even though such information is 'available upon request' in contrast with the GDPR (Article 43(2)(d)).

related to the integrity of the certification body related to lack of potential conflict of interest and respect of the data protection criteria of Articles 43(2)(b) and 43(2)(d).[46]

2.8 Oversight by the National Supervisory Authorities (Building Block 3)

The supervisory authorities have an active role in the EU data protection certification mechanism, being responsible for the oversight of the mechanism, and having the powers to 'intervene' in the result of the process. The final version of GDPR is influenced in that respect by the European Parliament proposal relating to the powers and tasks of the supervisory authorities in certification. Even though there are substantial differences in the aim and operation of the data protection mechanisms (instead of a unique European Data Protection Seal proposed by the Parliament), the supervisory authorities, as seen above, may intervene in several phases of the certification procedure and play a central role in the process. Usually, once accredited, the certification body is already deemed to have the expertise and integrity required to perform the certification procedure and reliably monitor the issued certification. In the case of the data protection certification mechanism of Articles 42 and 43, the supervisory authority performs periodic reviews of the issued certificates,[47] withdraws certificates and even has the power to *order* the certification body not to issue or not to renew a certification, if the requirements are not or no longer met.[48] The role of the supervisory authority reflects the aim of the regulator to add an additional layer of safeguards in the data protection certification mechanism. These powers and obligations of the supervisory authority raise questions of liability in cases of inaccurate, false or outdated certificates. In terms of reviewing of issued certificates, the supervisory authorities are obliged to perform periodic reviews, according to Article 57(1)(o).[49]

An issue that is not specified in the GDPR is the EU cross-border recognition of the data protection certification mechanisms. The GDPR describes national data protection certification mechanisms that are linked to the competent supervisory authorities of the Member States. There is no provision related to mandatory recognition of certifications, seals or marks and cooperation of the supervisory

---

[46] The accreditation by the supervisory authority is valid for a period of five years. Any revocation of accreditation by the National Accreditation Body is mandatory when the conditions for granting are not met (Article 43(4) GDPR).

[47] Article 57(1)(p) and Article 58(1)(c) GDPR.

[48] Article 58(2)(h) GDPR.

[49] Despite the existence of such obligation "where applicable", such an interpretation is in line with the aim of the legislator, who involves the supervisory authority in the procedure as an additional guarantee of the transparency and reliability of the data protection certification mechanism and certificate.

authorities in the field of certification, apart from the common certification offered by the European Data Protection Seal in line with the consistency mechanism. The silence of the GDPR can be problematic. This omission results in the scheme of *national* mechanisms based on *nationally approved* criteria derived from *EU* legislation, which is not far from the data protection seals as developed under the Data Protection Directive regime. Notwithstanding the value of national data protection certifications, marks and seals, and their benefit to support compliance and promote transparency in the data processing operations in the jurisdiction of each Member State, there are several arguments to support the view that such certifications should be recognised by the other supervisory authorities of Member States under the GDPR regime. If this is not the case, then the data controller or processor would need to undergo a certification process in each Member State in which the controller operates. The Privacy Bridges report highlighted the importance of certification as a means of accountability, organisational responsibility and compliance with the EU data protection law, but at the same time stressed the lack of wide pan-European acceptance of existing national certification schemes.[50] The multiplicity of national certifications, seals and marks, along with a European Data Protection Seal, could lead to market confusion if their differences are not clear to the data subjects.[51] This argument is also supported by Article 43(9) which provides the European Commission with the power to adopt implementing acts in line with Article 5 of the Regulation 182/2011 to lay down technical standards and mechanisms to promote and *recognise* the certification mechanisms, seals and marks.[52]

2.9 Register-Keeping and European Seal by the European Data Protection Board (Building Block 4)

The European Data Protection Board ("Board") is meant to replace the Article 29 Data Protection Working Party.[53] The Board will have legal personality[54] and its aim is to ensure the consistent application of the GDPR.[55] In this framework, the Board is involved with the data protection certification mechanism of Articles 42 and 43. In particular, the Board ensures transparency of the certification mechanism

---

[50] Privacy Bridges, EU and US Privacy Experts in search of transatlantic Privacy Solutions, September 2015, p. 16. https://privacybridges.mit.edu/sites/default/files/documents/PrivacyBridges-FINAL.pdf. Accessed 15 January 2017.

[51] Bennett argues that "Ironically, the more privacy seal programs there are, the more consumers will be confused, and the more difficult it will be for any one system to achieve a reputation as the methodology by which privacy protection practices can be claimed and assured". Bennett 2004, pp. 210–226.

[52] Regulation 182/2011 28.2.2011.

[53] Giurgiu et al. 2015, p. 17.

[54] Article 68(1) GDPR.

[55] Article 70(1) GDPR.

by keeping a *public register* with accredited bodies pursuant to paragraph of Article 43 and of the accredited controllers or processors established in third countries pursuant to para 7 of Article 42.[56] Moreover, the Board collects all the certification mechanisms and data protection seals in a register and makes them publicly available through any appropriate means.[57] Although the public register would probably entail extended coordination and resources on the part of the Board to organise and keep such a register up-to-date, the register offers the much-needed transparency for the data protection certifications.[58]

Regarding the European Data Protection Seal, the final version of the GDPR does not follow the European Parliament proposal on vision, structure and organisation of the Seal. The final GDPR version foresees a European Data Protection Seal, without including elaborate provisions. The only reference in the Regulation is in Article 42(5) in relation to the criteria of the Seal. The European Data Protection Board shall approve criteria for the data protection certification mechanism in the framework of the consistency mechanism of Article 63, a task that in the national data protection mechanisms is reserved for the supervisory authorities (Article 57(1)(n)). In such case, the GDPR provides that the criteria might lead to a "*common certification*". The Board has also the task of specifying requirements with a view to accreditation of certification bodies (Article 70(1)(p)). The common certification, it can be assumed, will be uniformly recognised by the supervisory authorities. For the operational issues of the Seal, the conditions of Article 43 would apply.

2.10 Criteria-Setting and the European Commission (Building Block 5)

As the EU privacy seals study showed,[59] a privacy seal scheme is as strong or weak as its criteria. The evaluation criteria are the backbone of the evaluation process, as each data processing activity is tested against the criteria in the framework of the certification process. Unlike seals or certification schemes in other fields that are based on diverse sources for their criteria, the criteria for the data protection certification mechanism under Article 42 will be based on the provisions of the General Data Protection Regulation. However, the high-level principles and general obligations of the GDPR need to be refined to be suitable for a certification process; by 'suitable', we mean that the evaluation criteria should not leave room for

---

[56] Article 70(1)(o) GDPR.

[57] Article 43(6) GDPR.

[58] In a survey conducted on security certification in the EU, 60.7% of the respondents replied that their most important need is that certification schemes are transparent in what they evaluate and certify. Read further on the identity of the survey and analysis, Kamara et al. 2015, p. 3.

[59] Rodrigues et al. 2014, p. 79.

subjective interpretation by the evaluators (auditors) of the certification body and they should be clear and precise. This is a challenging task, but necessary to achieve uniform objective and robust certification. It is important, therefore, that data protection certification schemes that are established pay good attention to the methodology of refining legal obligations and principles. As to the content of the criteria, the certification criteria could be influenced by the full text of the GDPR, including data processing principles (Article 5), conditions for lawfulness of processing (Article 6), type of personal data and specific conditions for processing (Article 9), rights of the data subject (Chapter III), technical and organisational measures of the data controller (Article 24), responsibilities of the processor (Article 28), security of processing (Article 32) and data transfers (Chapter V). The task is even more challenging considering the different sectors where such a certification or seal might be used. The technical and organisational measures needed in a cloud processor environment, for instance, are not identical to the technical and organisational measures in a hospital. The criteria need to strike the right balance between being flexible enough to accommodate such differences and clear enough to eliminate subjectivity from the evaluator side. Guidance at the Union level on the evaluation criteria is necessary, not only to assist the certification bodies to implement the criteria, but also to guide the supervisory authorities.

The process of *specifying* the evaluation criteria is ambiguous in the GDPR.[60] The only explicit reference in that respect is the *approval* of the criteria, which Article 42(5) provides is conducted by the *competent supervisory authority*, or in the case of the European Data Protection Seal, by the European Data Protection Board. An approval by the supervisory authority is a binding act, necessary for the use of the criteria in the data protection mechanism.[61] For the certification to be 'valid' (according to the GDPR), the certification decision needs to be established in accordance with the established (*approved*) criteria.[62] However, there is no direct reference on *who* drafts and proposes the evaluation criteria for approval. As

---

[60] The criteria are fundamental for a trusted, high-quality certification scheme. The schemes might involve procedural (for instance the object of the criterion might be on whether the organisation/product all relevant measures and policies relevant to a criterion) or results-based assessment criteria (for instance for a criterion data-security, the aim of the criterion is on the result, namely secure data, not focusing on how appropriate were the measures taken, as long as the result is achieved). Bock 2016, p. 337.

[61] The Article 29 Data Protection Working Party in its opinion 8/2012 providing input on the data protection reform discussions stated: "Since the certification mechanisms are to be encouraged in particular at European level, specifying further the criteria and requirements should be done on a European level as well. Since it would be hard to spell out all criteria and requirements in full in the text of the Regulation, it would be appropriate to adopt a more flexible instrument to provide further criteria and guidance for the data protection certification mechanisms, including conditions for granting and withdrawal and for requirements for recognition within the Union and in third countries. In order to ensure legal certainty towards the data subjects who rely on the certification mechanisms, seals and marks, a delegated act would indeed seem the most appropriate instrument.", Article 29 Data Protection Working Party 2012, p. 36.

[62] Albrecht 2016, p. 39.

opposed to the accreditation criteria, where the legislator explicitly entrusts the supervisory authorities to *draft* and *publish* the criteria for accreditation of the certification body (Article 57(1)(p)), in the case of evaluation criteria there is a lacuna. This lacuna can be interpreted by an intention of the regulator to allow *third parties,* such as certification bodies, to draft and propose criteria for approval by the supervisory authorities. The regulator indirectly urges the European Commission to undertake this task by adopting implementing acts that lay down technical standards for the data protection certification mechanisms, seals and marks (Article 43(9)).[63] However, since the adoption of implementing acts is at the discretion of the Commission, the drafting of criteria is open to other parties as well.

According to Article 43(8), the Commission shall *be empowered* to adopt delegated acts to specify the requirements for the data protection certification mechanisms of Article 42.[64] The GDPR refers to *requirements* 'to be taken into account for the data protection certification mechanisms'. The certification requirements of Article 43(8) are different from the evaluation criteria of Article 42(5),[65] and they must be seen as *complementary* requirements, which need to be taken into account when developing the data protection certification mechanism.[66] Delegated acts adopted by the Commission are subject to objection by the European Parliament and the Council before their entering into force[67] and offer the element of uniformity to the data protection mechanisms through requirements drafted at EU level.

2.11 Certification Effects: Voluntary, Not Binding for Data Protection Authorities and Regulated 'Benefits'

The data protection certification under GDPR is voluntary (Article 42(3)). The data controller or processor can demonstrate its compliance with its obligations stemming from the GDPR through certification and/or in any other way. There is no obligation in the GDPR for data controllers or processors to obtain such a certification. Thus, the voluntary nature of certification relates to the *decision* to submit

---

[63] Lachaud 2015, p. 6.

[64] See also Recital (166) on delegated acts.

[65] The GDPR does not provide a definition of 'criteria' nor 'requirements' in the data protection certification mechanism context. However, the GDPR differentiates the two terms in several articles, e.g. 43(2)(6).

[66] Recital 166 refers to delegated acts for both criteria *and* requirements. This wording remained the same in the relevant Recital across all versions of the GDPR and did not follow the abolition of the word 'criteria' in the relevant provision of Article 43 (previous Article 39a) which was made in the political agreement text of December 2015.

[67] Article 92(5) GDPR. In addition, Article 92(3) provides: "The delegation of power referred to in Article 12(8) and Article 43(8) may be revoked at any time by the European Parliament or by the Council."

oneself to the certification procedure and the *means* of demonstration of compliance to the legal obligations of the GDPR. In most certification application areas, certification is voluntary. There are a few exceptions such as the CE marking for safety of products traded in the European Economic Area (EEA) or mandatory certification in the construction sector.[68] Such markings however are often self-declaration of conformity mechanisms, which should be distinguished from the mechanism established in the GDPR.[69] In this case, the voluntary nature of the data protection certification is the correct solution. Certification of data processing may bring benefits to controllers and processors, but it might not be necessary in several cases, such as entities with limited data processing operations. Moreover, certification costs relating to the certification application, auditing, and renewal of the certification might be particularly high on some occasions and a controller or processor would need to assess the benefits of such certification in each individual case.

As stated, data protection certification mechanisms are "means to demonstrate compliance" with the GDPR. In relation to the binding effect, the regulator decided to state clearly the certification effect in terms of regulatory inspections and audits. Article 42(4) provides an explicit statement that the certification based on the GDPR does not reduce the responsibility of the controller or the processor for compliance with the GDPR. In other words, certification should not be viewed as offering a presumption of conformity with the legal obligations stemming from the GDPR. A completed certification procedure does *not* entail *prima facie* full compliance of the controller or processor with the GDPR. The controller or processor needs to take all necessary measures to comply with their obligations independently of any certification process or seal. The certification is a means of externalising in a concrete and objective way that technical and organisational measures (or a part of them depending on the scope of the certification) have been taken and implemented in a satisfactory manner. In addition, the supervisory authorities are not restrained from their powers in the cases of the controller of processor with a data protection certificate based on Article 42. The powers of the authorities to supervise the application of the GDPR and enforce its provisions remain intact.

Even though the final text does not go as far as to establish a binding, at least for the authorities, certification or seal, it does imply *benefits* in its Article 83 when such certification or seal exists. Article 83 on general conditions for imposing administrative fines provides that a supervisory authority, when deciding *whether* to impose an administrative fine and deciding on the *amount* of the administrative fine *should* give due regard on whether the controller or processor has adhered to approved data protection mechanisms of Article 42.[70] This provision can provide a strong motivation to controllers and processors to undergo the certification process

---

[68] Read Lachaud 2016, p. 149f on the shortcomings of using the CE marking in enforcing data protection and privacy in the Internet of Things.

[69] Mandatory third party certification is more commonly found at a national level, as it may be supported by national legislation. Read further: Consumer Research Associates Ltd. 2007.

[70] Article 83(2)(j) GDPR: "adherence to approved codes of conduct pursuant to Article 40 or approved certification mechanisms pursuant to Article 42".

of Article 42. In addition, a certification may be beneficial for controllers or processors when investigated by a supervisory authority.[71]

2.12 Functions and Possible Uses of Data Protection Certification in the GDPR

The use of certification, seals and marks of Articles 42 and 43 is not limited in terms of scope to specific provisions of the GDPR in the sense that the certificates can cover processing operations in relation to several sections of the GDPR.[72] In this section, we outline possible functions of the data protection certifications.

First, demonstrating accountability. As the Article 29 Working Party noted in its opinion on the principle of accountability, the provision on accountability may foster the development of certification programs or seals, as these programs would contribute to prove that a controller has implemented appropriate measures, which have been audited periodically.[73] The stated aim of data protection certification is to enhance transparency and demonstrate compliance with the obligations of the Regulation. These two elements are prominent manifestations of the accountability principle. The newly introduced principle of accountability (Article 5(2)), was long awaited to be part of the legal text, as in practice, the shift from mere compliance to accountability had already been landmarked. According to the principle of accountability, the data controller is responsible for complying with the principles of processing and should be able to demonstrate its compliance to the authorities. In comparison to the Data Protection Directive (95/46/EC), the controller not only has to comply, but also bears the burden of demonstrating compliance. Article 24 of the GDPR on the responsibility of the controller establishes the accountability framework. The data controller is obliged to implement technical and organisational measures to comply with the GDPR and demonstrate that the processing of personal data complies with the GDPR. In achieving this obligation, the controller should consider the nature, scope, context and purposes of the processing. In addition, two new elements that the controller should assess in taking the appropriate measures are the *risks* of and the *severity* for the rights and freedoms of individuals. Article 24 (3) explicitly provides that certification may be used as 'an element by which to demonstrate compliance with the obligations of the controller.' Thus, a data protection certification and seal will be assessed by the supervisory authority when examining the compliance of the controller with its obligations. The provision does

---

[71] See   Data   Protection   Authority   of   Bavaria   for   the   Private   Sector, 'EU-Datenschutz-Grundverordnung: Zertifizierung', June 2016, https://www.lda.bayern.de/media/baylda_ds-gvo_2_certification.pdf. Accessed 27 July 2016.

[72] On the issue of the object of certification, see ENISA 2017.

[73] Article 29 Data Protection Working Party 2010, p. 17f, http://ec.europa.eu/justice/policies/privacy/docs/wpdocs/2010/wp173_en.pdf. Accessed 4 July 2016.

not bind the supervisory authority to limit the enforcement when there is a data protection certificate or seal, but such a certificate or a seal would be one of the means at the disposal of the controller to demonstrate his or her compliance.[74] The Bavarian Data Protection Authority has stated in its guidance paper issued in 2016 that organisations applying for certification need to have good data protection management, good knowledge of their processing activities, and transparent documentation.

Second, demonstrating security of processing. Certification and technical standards have been developed and widely used in the field of information security.[75] In the context of Article 32 of the Regulation, the data controller and the processor shall implement technical and organisational measures to ensure security of processing. The Regulation provides a non-exhaustive list of measures such as pseudonymisation, encryption of personal data, confidentiality, integrity, availability and resilience of the systems and services processing personal data, timely restoration of availability and access to data in case of physical or technical accident, and an assessment process for the effectiveness of the measures.[76] Certification, as with the other provisions outlined in this section, can be used as an element to demonstrate compliance with the requirements of the relevant provision, in case the data protection mechanism includes security of processing criteria based on Article 30 GDPR.

Third, facilitating the choice of processors. Cloud computing and Internet of Things (IoT), where multiple processors are involved, stress the significance of a trustworthy processor. The data controller is obliged to have processors that provide sufficient guarantees for the compliance with the GDPR (Article 32). The GDPR establishes responsibility and liability of the controller for any processing carried out on his or her behalf by the processor.[77] Given the need for a controller to employ processors in different jurisdictions, a certified processor in line with the data protection mechanism of Article 42 would provide concrete evidence of due diligence from the part of the processor to comply with the GDPR.[78] In addition, the existence of such a data protection certificate or seal would be time and cost effective for the controller and facilitate its choice for processor. In case of damages caused by the processor, the controller could potentially benefit in terms of liability

---

[74] Bavarian Data Protection Authority for the Private Sector 2016.

[75] For instance, the Common Criteria standard ISO/IEC 15408 and certification. Read further: Rannenberg 2000, European Union Agency for Network and Information 2013. Also, ISO/IEC 27011:2013 Information technology—Security techniques—Information security management systems—Requirements, ISO/IEC 27002:2013 Information technology—Security techniques—Code of practice for information security controls, and ISO/IEC 27018:2014 Information technology—Security techniques—Code of practice for protection of personally identifiable information (PII) in public clouds acting as PII processors. De Hert et al. 2015.

[76] Article 32(1)(a)–(d) GDPR.

[77] Recital 74 GDPR.

[78] Recital 77 provides: "Adherence of the processor to an approved code of conduct or an approved certification mechanism may be used as an element to demonstrate compliance with the obligations of the controller."

from the selection of a certified processor, as this fact could be considered from a supervisory or judicial authority, in the framework of Article 82.[79]

Fourth, demonstrating compliance with the principle of 'Data protection by Design and by Default'. Article 25(1) and (2) set the framework for data protection by design and by default in the Regulation. The two principles are established under the Section of the Regulation on the obligations of the controller. The controller shall take appropriate technical and organisational measures that are designed to implement data protection principles, both at the time of the determination of the means of processing and the time of processing itself, to meet the requirements of the Regulation. Such measures should be implemented by default, meaning that the data subject is already protected from data protection risks.[80] The certification mechanism of Article 42 would be used to demonstrate compliance with the two obligations. In practice, there is already ongoing standardisation activity at European level based on the EU data protection legislation. The standardisation request 530 from the European Commission on privacy and personal data protection management in support of Union's security industrial policy[81] will provide European standard(s) addressing privacy management in the design and development and in the production and service provision processes of security technologies.[82] It would be preferable if such efforts, which involve translating data protection by design and by default into standardisation and certification requirements, would be coordinated to avoid opposing or contradictory results, since they are all initiated by public authorities; the European Commission in the case of the standardisation mandate and the supervisory authorities or the European Data Protection Board in the case of certification mechanisms of Article 42.[83]

Fifth, providing adequate safeguards for data transfers. In October 2015, the Court of Justice of the EU declared the invalidity of the Safe Harbour Decision.[84] Following the court ruling, there have been many discussions about the post-Safe Harbour regime,[85] which will enable the data transfers between the EU and the US, while safeguarding the data subject's rights and offering effective redress rights.[86] Data protection certification as in Article 42(2), might offer grounds for such transfers. Article 42(2) reads:

---

[79] Article 82 GDPR.

[80] Danezis et al. 2014, p. 5.

[81] M/530 Commission Implementing Decision 2015.

[82] Kamara 2017.

[83] The M/530 explicitly refers to the EC proposal for a General Data Protection Regulation and a "data protection by default and by design" approach (Recital 3).

[84] Judgment in Case C-362/14 Maximillian Schrems v Data Protection Commissioner, ECLI:EU: C:2015:650.

[85] Read, among others, Kuner 2015.

[86] On 2 February 2016, the Commission and US competent authorities reached an agreement on a new framework enabling transatlantic data flows, the EU-US Privacy Shield. Statement from the EC of 2 February 2016, http://europa.eu/rapid/press-release_IP-16-216_en.htm. Accessed 18 January 2017.

In addition to adherence by controllers or processors subject to this Regulation, data protection certification mechanisms, seals or marks approved pursuant to paragraph 5 of this Article may be established for the purpose of demonstrating the existence of appropriate safeguards provided by **controllers or processors that are not subject to this Regulation** pursuant to Article 3 within the framework of **personal data transfers to third countries or international organisations** under the terms referred to in point (f) of Article 46(2). Such controllers or processors shall **make binding and enforceable commitments, via contractual or other legally binding instruments**, to apply those appropriate safeguards, including with regard to the rights of the data subjects.[87] [emphasis added]

The provisions on data transfers (Article 44) include the data protection certification mechanisms of Article 42(2) as one of the instruments to provide "appropriate safeguards" for data transfers in the absence of an adequacy decision by the European Commission.[88] Approved certification mechanisms belong in the category of instruments providing appropriate safeguards *without requiring any specific authorisation from a supervisory authority.* Binding corporate rules,[89] standard data protection clauses[90] and approved codes of conduct are in the same category.[91] The legislator also requires that the certified controller or processor makes enforceable commitments *in the third country* to apply the appropriate safeguards, including with regard to data subjects' rights.[92] As explicitly stated in Article 42, the provision on data transfers based on certification, concerns also controllers and processors who are not subject to the Regulation (Article 3). The novel provision opens the gates for data flows without the need for ad hoc authorisation by the data protection authority with the sole possession of a data protection certification and enforceable commitments from the controller or processor. The provision, which might be particularly attractive and motivating for controllers and processors, has potential serious legal consequences for the data subjects. The above quoted Article 42(2) requires "binding and enforceable commitments, via contractual or other legally binding instruments". Such commitments, even if considered as binding by the national legislation of the third country and supported by an appropriate judicial system (e.g. materially competent courts for such cases), would be almost impossible to be enforced by the data subjects themselves. In such contracts and agreements, the data subjects are not parties; therefore, in principle they do not have enforceable rights. For the controllers and processors subject to the GDPR, Article 82(1) establishing the right to compensation for data subjects from material or immaterial damage would apply.

---

[87] Article 42(2) GDPR.

[88] Article 45 GDPR.

[89] Article 46(2)(b) GDPR.

[90] Article 46(2)(c)(d) GDPR.

[91] Article 46(2)(e) GDPR.

[92] Article 46(2)(e) GDPR.

2.13 Next Steps and Reflections on Risks and the Potential of the New System

This chapter presents the data protection certification mechanism in Articles 42 and 43 of the GDPR. The new data protection framework embraces co-regulation by establishing third-party audited certification mechanisms. In relation to the European Commission Proposal, which only encouraged certification, the final text is an upgrade, as it contains vision, function, process and general requirements for the data protection certification mechanism. In relation to the Parliament vision, one cannot ignore the differences between the certification models of the Parliament first reading and the final text of the GDPR: a strong binding EU common data protection seal granted by the supervisory authorities on the one hand (EP), and multiple national certification mechanisms granted by accredited third party (certification bodies) auditors on the other hand. The Parliament model is primarily aimed at protecting the data subject rights and enhancing transparency in the data processing of certified controllers and processors. It could be said that the lack of maturity of the (data protection) certification market, the data protection authorities in terms of relevant expertise and resources, and the newly established European Data Protection Board, would not allow a wide adoption of the European Data Protection Seal or at least the full development of the potential of such a strong pan-European seal operated by public authorities.

The final text opted for a more conscious choice in that respect, showing awareness of the above issues. Articles 42 and 43 do not disregard the accumulated experience of established public National Accreditation Bodies, accredited certification bodies (that may have experience in areas such as cloud computing, information security, radio frequency identification or RFID and others) and broadly-used technical standards. The regulator calls the existing certification ecosystem to take part in the data protection certification mechanism. To ensure a high level of protection of the data subject rights and safeguard against non-transparent, fraudulent or deceptive cases, the regulator empowers supervisory authorities with significant powers to accredit, approve criteria, issue, review, renew and withdraw certificates. This is a significant improvement on the Council version, which for instance did not foresee a binding decision of the supervisory authorities on the certification criteria. Despite the differences in the models of Article 42[93] in the versions of the Regulation, the final text keeps the European Data Protection Seal vision alive, by referring to the common certification mechanism and the European Data Protection Board. This provision is potentially promising for future consideration, once the Board is well established and there is already experience from the national data protection mechanisms based on the GDPR.

One point of criticism is the lack of definitions and distinction of certifications, seals and marks. An additional point of criticism of the new system would be that

---

[93] Previously Article 39 of the European Commission Proposal, European Parliament and Council first reading.

the decision to grant the certification or seal (attestation stage) together with the issue should be under the final approval or full responsibility of the supervisory authorities, based on the evaluation results (reports) of the certification body. With the current status of the GDPR certification provisions, particular attention should be given to strict requirements for accreditation, to ensure that the certification body will deliver sound results of undisputable quality. Regarding the certification criteria-setting, the ambiguous wording in the GDPR with regard to which entity drafts the criteria, might lead to a diverse landscape of data protection certification mechanisms across the EU. Implementing and delegated acts of the European Commission specifying requirements that need to be taken into account for the data protection mechanisms could play a role in that respect, even though in general, the choice of the instrument of delegated acts for specifying the requirements has been criticised as leaving "data controllers and data processors uncertain of their obligations" and seriously impeding "long-term business planning since the rules could be changed at any time".[94]

As stressed in this chapter, the benefits and uses of the data protection certification, seals and marks are manifold. Certification can be used to demonstrate compliance with the GDPR, specifically data protection by design and by default, security of processing, processor providing sufficient guarantees and accountability. From the perspective of the data protection authorities, the Bavarian Data Protection Authority highlights that the GDPR certification may have great potential to clarify whether the statutory data protection requirements are respected.[95] In addition, the Authority notes the potential benefit of certification to help better understand the level of compliance in certain cases, such as for instance, cloud computing.[96] Certification mechanisms along with binding and enforceable commitments can also be the grounds for adequate safeguards for data transfers, when there is no adequacy decision from the EC. This provision provides new perspective for the data protection certification of the EU as facilitator of data flows outside the EU. However, since the impact on data subject rights which are at stake with such flows is particularly high, the task of careful consideration of both the accreditation and certification processes and the setting of strict requirements and surveillance of the accredited bodies and issued certificates is of utmost significance. Guidance at EU level will be needed to ensure the harmonised application of Articles 42 and 43 of the Regulation.

Certification and seals are a means to promote transparency of processes of controllers and processors and aid accountable organisations to demonstrate how they comply with the GDPR. Despite the regular criticism against such efforts as

---

[94] Kosta and Stuurman 2016, p. 458.
[95] Data Protection Authority of Bavaria for the Private Sector 2016.
[96] Ibid.

'soft' measures, their legal effect should not be underrated; certification in the form of third-party audits and certification agreements has enforceable legal effects.

Acknowledgements The research for this contribution is partially based on research conducted in the framework of the FP7 CRISP project (grant agreement 607941). The views expressed in this chapter are the authors' alone. They would like to thank Dick Hortensius for his valuable feedback on a previous version of the chapter.

References

Abramatic J-F et al (2015) Privacy Bridges, EU and US Privacy Experts in Search of Transatlantic Privacy Solutions. Available at: https://privacybridges.mit.edu/

Albrecht J P (2016) The EU's New Data Protection Law – How A Directive Evolved Into A Regulation; Overview of the designated final text of the EU's General Data Protection Regulation, and consideration of the background to it, after the Agreement in the Trilogue. Computer Law Review International, Issue 2 April 2016

Article 29 Data Protection Working Party (2016) Statement on the 2016 action plan for the implementation of the General Data Protection Regulation (GDPR) WP236. http://ec.europa.eu/justice/data-protection/article-29/documentation/opinion-recommendation/files/2016/wp236_en.pdf. Accessed 3 February 2016

Article 29 Data Protection Working Party (2012) Opinion 08/2012 providing further input on the data protection reform discussions. WP199, October 5, 2012

Article 29 Data Protection Working Party (2010) Opinion 03/2010 on the principle of Accountability, WP173, July 2010

Bennett C J (2004) Privacy Self-Regulation in a Global Economy: A Race to the Top, the Bottom or Somewhere Else? Voluntary Codes: Private Governance, the Public Interest and Innovation. Carleton University, Ottawa, 210–226

Bock K (2016) Data Protection Certification: Decorative or Effective Instrument? Audit and Seals as a Way to Enforce Privacy. In: Wright D, De Hert P (eds) Enforcing Privacy Regulatory, Legal and Technological Approaches. Springer, Heidelberg

Consumer Research Associates Ltd (2007) EFTA Study on Certification and Marks in Europe. Study commissioned by the European Free Trade Association (EFTA), December 2007. http://www.efta.int/sites/default/files/publications/study-certification-marks/executive-summary.pdf. Accessed 29 February 2016

Danezis G et al (2014) Privacy and Data Protection by Design– from policy to engineering. ENISA. https://www.enisa.europa.eu/activities/identity-and-trust/library/deliverables/privacy-and-data-protection-by-design. Accessed 29 February 2016

Data Protection Authority of Bavaria for the Private Sector (2016) EU-Datenschutz Grundverordnung: Zertifizierung, June 2016

De Hert P et al (2014) Challenges and Possible Scope of an EU Privacy Seal Scheme. D.3.3 Final Report for Privacy Seals Study, January 2014

De Hert P et al (2015) The cloud computing standard ISO/IEC 27018 through the lens of the EU legislation on data protection. Computer Law and Security Review (32):16–30

EC DG Justice (2010) Comparative Study on Different Approaches to new Privacy Challenges, in particular in the light of technological Developments. Final Report, 20 January 2010. http://ec.europa.eu/justice/policies/privacy/docs/studies/new_privacy_challenges/final_report_en.pdf. Accessed 28 February 2016

ENISA (2017) Recommendations on European Data Protection Certification, version 1.0, November 2017. https://www.enisa.europa.eu/publications/recommendations-on-european-data-protection-certification. Accessed 18 December 2017

European Commission (2010) Communication from the Commission of 19 May 2010 to the European Parliament, the Council, the European Economic and Social Committee and the Committee of the Regions – A Digital Agenda for Europe [COM(2010) 245 final – Not published in the Official Journal]. http://eur-lex.europa.eu/legal-content/EN/TXT/?uri= URISERV%3Asi0016. Accessed 10 December 2015

European Commission (2012) Proposal for a Regulation of the European Parliament and of the Council on the protection of individuals with regard to the processing of personal data and on the free movement of such data (General Data Protection Regulation) COM (2012) 11 final – 2012/0011 (COD), 25.01.2012

European Commission, High Representative of the European Union for Foreign Affairs and Security Policy (2013) Joint Communication to the European Parliament, the Council, the European Economic and Social Committee and the Committee of the Regions Cybersecurity Strategy of the European Union: An Open, Safe and Secure Cyberspace. JOIN(2013) 1 final

European Commission (2015) M/530 Commission Implementing Decision C (2015) 102 final of 20.1.2015 on a standardisation request to the European standardisation organisations as regards European standards and European standardisation deliverables for privacy and personal data protection management pursuant to Article 10(1) of Regulation (EU) No 1025/2012 of the European Parliament and of the Council in support of Directive 95/46/EC of the European Parliament and of the Council and in support of Union's security industrial policy. ftp:// ftp.cencenelec.eu/CENELEC/EuropeanMandates/M530_EN.pdf. Accessed 28 February 2016

European Council (2015) Preparation of a general approach. 9565/15, 11.6.2015, adopted at JHA Council Meeting on 15.6.2015

European Parliament and Council (1995) Directive 95/46/EC of the European Parliament and of the Council of 24 October 1995 on the protection of individuals with regard to the processing of personal data and on the free movement of such data (Data Protection Directive). OJ L 281, 23.11.1995

European Parliament and Council (2008) Regulation (EC) No 765/2008 of the European Parliament and of the Council of 9 July 2008 setting out the requirements for accreditation and market surveillance relating to the marketing of products and repealing Regulation (EEC) No 339/93. OJ L 218/30, 13.8.2008

European Parliament and the Council (2002) Directive 2002/58/EC of the European Parliament and of the Council of 12 July 2002 concerning the processing of personal data and the protection of privacy in the electronic communications sector (Directive on privacy and electronic communications). OJ L 201, 31.7.2002

European Parliament and the Council (2009) Directive 2009/136/EC of the European Parliament and of the Council of 25 November 2009 amending Directive 2002/22/EC on universal service and users' rights relating to electronic communications networks and services, Directive 2002/ 58/EC concerning the processing of personal data and the protection of privacy in the electronic communications sector and Regulation (EC) No 2006/2004 on cooperation between national authorities responsible for the enforcement of consumer protection laws. OJ L 337/11, 18.12.2009

European Parliament and Council of the European Union (2013) Regulation (EU) No 182/2011 of the European Parliament and of the Council of 16 February 2011 laying down the rules and general principles concerning mechanisms for control by Member States of the Commission's exercise of implementing powers. OJ L 55/13, 28.2.2011

European Parliament (2014) Legislative resolution of 12 March 2014 on the proposal for a regulation of the European Parliament and of the Council on the protection of individuals with regard to the processing of personal data and on the free movement of such data (General Data Protection Regulation). (COM(2012)0011 – C7-0025/2012 – 2012/0011(COD))

European Parliament and Council of the European Union, Regulation (2016) 2016/679 of the European Parliament and of the Council of 27 April 2016 on the protection of natural persons with regard to the processing of personal data and on the free movement of such data, and repealing Directive 95/46/EC (General Data Protection Regulation), L 119/1 4.5.2016

European Union Agency for Network and Information Security (ENISA) (2013) Security framework Guidelines for trust services providers – Part 1.Version 1.0. https://www.enisa. europa.eu/activities/identity-and-trust/trust-services/guidelines-tsp. Accessed 28 February 2016

Federal Trade Commission (2015) FTC Approves Final Order In TRUSTe Privacy Case. https:// www.ftc.gov/news-events/press-releases/2015/03/ftc-approves-final-order-truste-privacy-case. Accessed 28 February 2016

Giurgiu A et al (2015) EU's One-Stop-Shop Mechanism: Thinking Transnational. Privacy Laws & Business: International Reports (137): 16–18

Graham G (2012) Global data privacy in a networked world. In: Brown I (ed) Research Handbook on Governance of the Internet. Edward Elgar, Cheltenham

Hustinx P (2008) The Role of Data Protection Authorities. Cahiers du Centre de Recherches Informatique et Droit (CRID) nr 31, Défis du droit à la protection de la vie privée / Challenges of privacy and data protection law. Namur-Bruxelles (2008): 561–568

Järvinen H (2015) Press Release: Privacy and Data Protection under threat from EU Council agreement. https://edri.org/. Accessed 28 February 2016

Judgment in Case C-362/14 Maximillian Schrems v Data Protection Commissioner

Kamara I (2017) Co-regulation in EU personal data protection: The case of technical standards and the privacy by design standardisation 'mandate'. European Journal of Law and Technology, Vol 8, No 1

Kamara I et al (2015) Raising trust in security products and systems through standardisation and certification: The CRISP approach. ITU Kaleidoscope: Trust in the Information Society (K-2015), IEEE Xplore (2015):1–7

Korff D (2014) Warning: the EU Council is Trying to Undermine Privacy Seals (and through this, the General Data Protection Regulation). EU Law Analysis Blog, 3 October 2014. http:// eulawanalysis.blogspot.nl/2014/10/warning-eu-council-is-trying-to.html. Accessed 28 February 2016

Kosta E, Stuurman K (2016) Technical standards and the draft General Data Protection Regulation. In: Delimatsis P (ed) The law, economics and politics of international standardization. Cambridge University Press, 434–460

Kuner C (2015) The Sinking of the Safe Harbor. Verfassungsblog of Constitutional Matters. http:// verfassungsblog.de/the-sinking-of-the-safe-harbor/. Accessed 28 February 2016

Lachaud E (2016) Could the CE Marking Be Relevant to Enforce Privacy by Design in the Internet of Things? In: Gutwirth S et al (eds) Current developments in ICT and Privacy/Data Protection. Springer, Heidelberg

Lachaud E (2015) Is Article 39 of the GDPR Suitable? SSRN: http://ssrn.com/abstract=2620214. Accessed 18 November 2015

Rannenberg K (2000) IT Security Certification and Criteria. In: Sihan Q (ed.) Information Security for Global Information Infrastructures. Kluwer Academic Publishers, Alphen aan den Rijn, 1–10

Rodrigues R et al (2014) Proposals and evaluation of policy options. Final Report Study Deliverable 4.4. EU Privacy Seals Project. http://publications.jrc.ec.europa.eu/repository/ bitstream/JRC91532/lbna26834enn.pdf. Accessed 28 February 2017

Rodrigues R, Barnard-Wills D, De Hert P, Papakonstantinou V (2016) The future of privacy certification in Europe: An exploration of options under article 42 of the GDPR. International Review of Law, Computers & Technology

Wright D et al (2015) Findings and Recommendations. Deliverable 4 for the PHAEDRA project. http://www.phaedra-project.eu/wp-content/uploads/Findings-and-recommendations-18-Jan-2015.pdf. Accessed 10 February 2017

Chapter 3
The Schleswig-Holstein Data Protection Seal

Marit Hansen

Contents

Abstract This chapter describes the Schleswig-Holstein Data Protection Seal. This trust mark for IT products is based on legal provisions introduced in the German State of Schleswig-Holstein in 2000. After explaining the legal provisions and the certification procedure of the Schleswig-Holstein Data Protection Seal, the chapter discusses its evolution. Further, it presents lessons learnt from the experience with the seal.

Keywords data protection · privacy · data protection seal · privacy seal · Schleswig-Holstein data protection seal · data protection authority

Marit Hansen, Data Protection Commissioner Schleswig-Holstein, Holstenstr. 98, 24103 Kiel, Germany, marit.hansen@datenschutzzentrum.de.

M. Hansen (✉)
Holstenstr. 98, 24103 Kiel, Germany
e-mail: marit.hansen@datenschutzzentrum.de

© T.M.C. ASSER PRESS and the authors 2018
R. Rodrigues and V. Papakonstantinou (eds.), *Privacy and Data Protection Seals*,
Information Technology and Law Series 28, https://doi.org/10.1007/978-94-6265-228-6_3

3.1   Introduction

The *Schleswig-Holstein Data Protection Seal* ("Datenschutz-Gütesiegel Schleswig-Holstein")[1] is one of the oldest privacy and data protection seals based on a law, namely, the State Data Protection Act of the German federal State Schleswig-Holstein.[2] It was created by the former Data Protection Commissioner of Schleswig-Holstein in the year 2002. The certification body for the *Schleswig-Holstein Data Protection Seal* is the office of the Data Protection Commissioner, i.e. the "Unabhängiges Landeszentrum für Datenschutz (ULD)" (translated as "Independent Centre for Privacy Protection").[3] The *Schleswig-Holstein Data Protection Seal* primarily addresses vendors of IT products, providing an incentive for compliance with data protection requirements. These requirements are derived from the applicable law and cover both legal and technological issues concerning data protection.

Schleswig-Holstein is the northernmost State (Land) of Germany. It is situated south of Denmark and north of Hamburg, having the Northern Sea in the west and the Baltic Sea in the east.

The Federal Republic of Germany consists of 16 States (Länder). The German constitution guarantees sovereignty of each Land in many political areas (e.g. police or education) while others are the exclusive responsibility of the federation (e.g. foreign affairs or defence). According to the European data protection law, both the federation and each of the Länder have to appoint an independent Data Protection Commissioner. When the European Data Protection Directive 95/46/EC came into effect, not only the German Federal Data Protection Act,[4] but also the State Data Protection Act of each Land had to comply with the Directive. Since the Länder are independent as regards law-making, their Data Protection Acts differ. In Schleswig-Holstein, the law-makers discussed the need to bring local law in line with European law with the Data Protection Commissioner Dr. Helmut Bäumler and his staff. The objective was not only to implement the provisions of the European Data Protection Directive, but also to reform the data protection law, which resulted in the State Data Protection Act of Schleswig-Holstein as applicable from 1 July 2000. Among others, this act contains provisions on two kinds of certifications: (1) a so-called "audit" of public authorities that ask the Data Protection Authority for a check of their data protection strategy ("Datenschutzkonzept") and can be awarded an audit seal, and (2) a certification of IT products after compliance with data protection requirements has been evaluated and determined. The latter is the focus of this text. The chapter is organised as follows: Section 3.2 describes the legal basis

---

[1] Since the *Schleswig-Holstein Data Protection Seal* mainly addresses the German market, most information on the seal is available in the German language; a few documents have been translated into English. See https://www.datenschutzzentrum.de/guetesiegel/. Accessed 27 April 2017.

[2] Schleswig-Holsteinisches Gesetz zum Schutz personenbezogener Informationen (Landesdatenschutzgesetz—LDSG) In Schleswig-Holstein GVOBl. 169, 204-42000.

[3] https://www.datenschutzzentrum.de/. Accessed 27 April 2017.

[4] Bundesdatenschutzgesetz (BDSG). In BGBl. I 66 2003.

for the *Schleswig-Holstein Data Protection Seal*. Section 3.3 explains its certification procedure. Section 3.4 briefly illustrates the evolution of the seal since the end of 2002. Section 3.5 discusses lessons learnt from the perspective of a Data Protection Authority as certification body. Finally, some conclusions are drawn in Sect. 3.6.

3.2 The Legal Provisions Supporting the Schleswig-Holstein Data Protection Seal

§ 4 of the State Data Protection Act Schleswig-Holstein was introduced to stress the importance of pivotal aspects of data protection by design for IT products: § 4 para 1 calls for data avoidance and data minimisation. § 4 para 2 addresses a so-called "data protection audit" and states:

> (2) Preference shall be given to products whose conformity with the data protection and data security provisions have been established by means of a formal procedure. The State Government shall make orders regulating the content and format of the procedure and who is authorised to carry it out.

The State Data Protection Act Schleswig-Holstein from 2000 thereby contains a provision for the "data protection audit" where further details shall be regulated in a by-law. This by-law is the Data Protection Seal Decree of Schleswig-Holstein ("Landesverordnung über ein Datenschutzgütesiegel (Datenschutzgütesiegelverordnung—DSGSVO").[5] It describes the formal procedure of the *Schleswig-Holstein Data Protection Seal*.

Due to the legal limitation of the State Data Protection Act Schleswig-Holstein to (1) the State of Schleswig-Holstein and (2) the public service, only IT products (software, hardware or automated processes) can be awarded such a data protection seal if they are suitable for use by the Schleswig-Holstein public service. Note that it is not necessary that the product is actually used by the Schleswig-Holstein public service, only its suitability has to be checked. This does not mean that the IT product has to be a special development for public service tasks, even the general functionality of a computer system could undergo certification.

Another important aspect of § 4 para 2 of the State Data Protection Act Schleswig-Holstein should be noted: The successful certification has to be considered in public procurement as "preference shall be given" to such certified IT products. This is a clear incentive for the vendors, and for the data controllers who have to ensure that the legal provisions are fulfilled when introducing a new IT

---

[5] The latest version from 30.11.2013 was published in Schleswig-Holstein GVOBl. 536, 204-4-7 2013.

product for their application context. The State Data Protection Act Schleswig-Holstein and an additional decree[6] demand from the data controller documentation, tests, and approval for each automated process. This task is significantly supported by a proof of conformity with data protection and data security provisions which is provided by each IT product that has been awarded the *Schleswig-Holstein Data Protection Seal*.

Some of the other State Data Protection Acts in Germany and the Federal Data Protection Act point to compliance audits and a potential data protection seal which could be regulated in an additional decree, but up until 2016 only the Data Protection Commission of Mecklenburg-Vorpommern has begun providing an own Data Protection Seal,[7] which is realised in cooperation with a company specialised in audits, the EuroPriSe GmbH.[8] This company is a spin-off of the European Privacy Seal initiative that was led by the Schleswig-Holstein Data Protection Authority until the end of 2013 before it was transferred to the newly founded company EuroPriSe GmbH.[9] Because of the relationship between the Schleswig-Holstein Data Protection Seal and EuroPriSe, the Mecklenburg Data Protection Seal is quite similar to the Schleswig-Holstein Seal.

3.3   The Certification Procedure of the Schleswig-Holstein Data Protection Seal

The following roles are evident in the Schleswig-Holstein Data Protection Seal certification procedure:

- The **applicant** applies for the seal for the Target of Evaluation (or ToE, i.e., the IT product in question) and chooses from a list of admitted experts who will perform the evaluation.
- **Admitted experts** perform the evaluation from both the legal and technical perspectives, and generate a report.
- The **admission board** admits experts who apply for admission and prove that they fulfil the admission criteria.

---

[6] Landesverordnung über die Sicherheit und Ordnungsmäßigkeit automatisierter Verarbeitung personenbezogener Daten (Datenschutzverordnung – DSVO), published in GVOBl. 554, 204-4-8 2013.

[7] https://www.datenschutz-mv.de/datenschutz/guetesiegel/guetesiegel.html (German). Accessed 27 April 2017.

[8] EuroPriSe Press Release 2014 "EuroPriSe starts work as certification authority for the privacy seal of German federal state Mecklenburg-Vorpommern", https://www.european-privacy-seal.eu/AppFile/GetFile/0d05a4f9-05ec-49af-9319-528bfc94564d. Accessed 27 April 2017. See footnote 7.

[9] ULD Press Release 2013 "ULD press release concerning further development of EuroPriSe", https://www.european-privacy-seal.eu/AppFile/GetFile/a1d64775-9d3d-4dd4-b46c-012131aed93f. Accessed 27 April 2017.

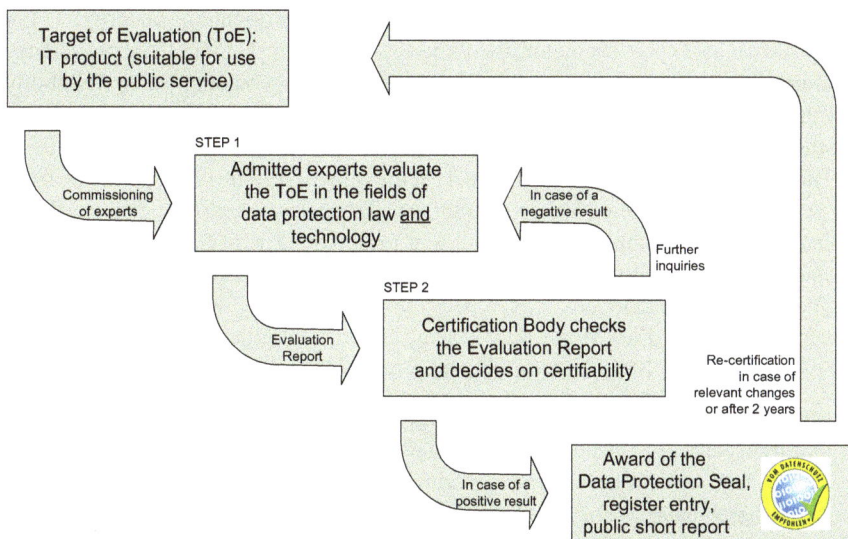

Fig. 3.1 Process of the Schleswig-Holstein Data Protection Seal [Source: M. Hansen]

- The **certification body** checks the report generated by the admitted experts with respect to the certifiability of the ToE. If the ToE is certifiable, the certification body awards the *Schleswig-Holstein Data Protection Seal*.

According to the Data Protection Seal Decree of Schleswig-Holstein, the ULD (the Data Protection Authority of Schleswig-Holstein) functions both as the admission board and the certification body.

The procedure is defined as follows (see also Fig. 3.1):[10] To begin the process of being awarded the *Schleswig-Holstein Data Protection Seal*, a manufacturer or vendor (applicant) of an IT product applies for the seal. The applicant selects evaluators from a published list of experts who have been admitted by the ULD.[11] Prior to the evaluation, the applicant and the experts conclude a contract that defines the ToE, the work to be done, and the price. In the public list of experts, fields of their expertise can be specified to be considered in the selection of the applicants. The admission criteria have been defined by the ULD when creating the *Schleswig-Holstein Data Protection Seal*, taking into account national and international guidelines, such as ISO 17025, and other certification schemes, e.g. the

---

[10] For more information see https://www.datenschutzzentrum.de/guetesiegel/ (German) or the leaflet "Seal of privacy for IT-products and privacy protection audit for public authorities" (English), https://www.datenschutzzentrum.de/uploads/guetesiegel/Seal-of-privacy-and-privacy-protection-audit.pdf. Accessed 27 April 2017.

[11] https://www.datenschutzzentrum.de/guetesiegel/register-sachverstaendige/ (German). Accessed 27 April 2017.

certification from the German Federal Office for Information Security.[12] For admission as an expert evaluator, the experts need to substantiate their proficiency regarding legal and/or technical qualifications on data protection, their reliability and their independence. The ULD can revoke the admission if the conditions are not met.

The admitted experts have to conduct their evaluation of the ToE on the basis of the published catalogue of *Schleswig-Holstein Data Protection Seal* criteria.[13] The evaluation always comprises both legal and technical expertise, often provided by not only one expert alone, but by a team of specialised experts.

The criteria catalogue developed by the ULD when creating the Schleswig-Holstein Data Protection Seal by deriving requirements from data protection law consists of four major criteria groups:[14]

1. Fundamental design aspects of the IT product (in particular, data minimisation and transparency) for built-in data protection,
2. Lawfulness of data processing covering the demand for identifying the appropriate legal basis (e.g., a law governing data processing or the individuals' consent),
3. Technical-organisational measures to exclude, or at least minimise, the risks of breaches and prevent security vulnerabilities,
4. Data subjects' rights, i.e., the right to access, the right to rectification, the right to erasure, the rights to blocking of data, the right to give or withdraw consent, the right to object (see e.g., the Data Protection Directive 95/46/EC).

The criteria catalogue has been elaborated by deriving the legal, technical and organisational requirements from potentially applicable data protection law. This comprises regulations issued at the State level of Schleswig-Holstein (State Data Protection Act, laws governing the public sector), at the Federal level of Germany (e.g., Federal Data Protection Act, Telemedia Law, Telecommunication Law, Social Act), from the German Constitution, and at the European level (Data Protection Directive 95/46/EC, e-Privacy Directive 2002/58/EC). Further, the Article 29 Data Protection Working Party's opinions are regularly considered while updating the criteria.

From this catalogue, admitted experts have to choose all criteria relevant to the ToE and its field of application as the basis of their evaluation. This encompasses:

- the legal framework, i.e., the set of potentially applicable laws and other regulation,
- the data types and data flows to understand how sensitive the data are and which roles may have access to the data,

---

[12] https://www.bsi.bund.de/EN/Topics/Certification/certification_node.html. Accessed 27 April 2017.

[13] https://www.datenschutzzentrum.de/download/anford.pdf (German). Accessed 27 April 2017.

[14] Hansen and Probst 2002.

- the intended usage and purposes, e.g., the primary functionality of the IT product or otherwise secondary purposes, e.g., for audits or for security reasons,
- the implementation, i.e., the functioning IT product including the documentation, and
- the technical environment, e.g., the platform or interfaces to other technical components.

For similar ToE and their field of application, the choice of relevant criteria will be similar. Therefore, it is possible to define "protection profiles" as termed in the Common Criteria for Information Technology Security Evaluation,[15] i.e. structured templates of criteria that can be applied for a group of ToEs.

The criteria must be applied to all subsystems of the IT product with potential privacy and data protection relevance. For instance, processes concerning logging and the handling of log files are usually a mandatory part of the evaluation. Thus, usage data, statistical data, data for authorisation or configuration data must be taken into account as well.

The admitted experts generate an evaluation report with their findings and submit it to the ULD, which checks the report and possibly the IT product itself. In the majority of cases, the first submission of the evaluation report does not enable a clear "pass" regarding the certifiability of the ToE because several issues might have to be clarified, or documentation to make the application's use compliant with the requirements might need to be added. In such cases, the applicant and the admitted experts are asked to respond to further inquiries and generate an improved revised version of the evaluation report.

If the ULD approves the legal and technical evaluation, the *Schleswig-Holstein Data Protection Seal* is awarded (certification). In general, it has a validity of two years. When creating the *Schleswig-Holstein Data Protection Seal*, it was discussed how long the validity should be regarding quick changes in IT products and their data protection and security properties on one hand, and the need for a minimum period of validity that is worth investing in a certification process, on the other hand. The period of two years has proven a proper balance of these requirements. If there are changes in the ToE, and this is not covered by the previous certification, the product must be re-evaluated. Re-certification is possible if a new evaluation is successfully conducted and approved. Usually a re-certification entails less effort than the first certification because the applicants make sure that the proper documentation is in place and that the developers consider the relevant criteria throughout the design and improvement process.

Revocation of the *Schleswig-Holstein Data Protection Seal* may occur if it turns out that the certified IT product is not compliant with the applicable data protection and data security provisions. Until now no certification has had to be revoked, but in several cases, especially when vulnerabilities of IT components became known—this is monitored by the certification body—or when people notified the

---

[15] https://www.commoncriteriaportal.org/. Accessed 27 April 2017. For the protection profiles of the Common Criteria, see https://www.commoncriteriaportal.org/pps/. Accessed 27 April 2017.

ULD team about potential risks, the certification body asked the applicants whether necessary changes were applied because otherwise a revocation would be deemed necessary.

The public *Schleswig-Holstein Data Protection Seal* Register[16] lists all certifications by assigning a unique register number, the name of the IT product including a version number, the application field of the product, the date of certification, the validity of the *Schleswig-Holstein Data Protection Seal,* and a link to a short evaluation report. The register also contains certifications that are no longer valid, whether expired or revoked (note, till the end of 2016 no certification had been revoked). The public report is a summary of the full evaluation report. While the full report may contain internal information (e.g., security-relevant data or business secrets), the short report describes among others the target of evaluation, the main aspects of the certification, potential issues, and exemplary functionality of the IT product and how it promotes privacy and data protection. The short reports are important for those who may be interested in using or buying the IT products because the existence of the awarded data protection seal does not contain sufficient information on the exact definition of the ToE and the evaluated properties. Also, some reports contain roadmaps for further improvements of the IT products which bind the manufacturers. The section on how the IT product promotes privacy and data protection can be employed by data protection authorities to use it as measure when evaluating other products. This contributes to enhancing the state-of-the-art.

3.4   Evolution of the Schleswig-Holstein Data Protection Seal

Since the end of 2002 when the ULD started with the *Schleswig-Holstein Data Protection Seal*, 96 IT products have been awarded the seal. To this day (November 2016), 44 of these IT products have successfully undergone at least one re-certification process, 22 IT products at least two re-certifications, and for 13 IT products three or more re-certifications have been performed.[17]

During the period of providing the *Schleswig-Holstein Data Protection Seal*, the criteria catalogue has been reviewed and updated a few times by the ULD team based on the feedback from applicants, admitted experts, other data protection authorities and stakeholders. This has taken place to accommodate changes in the State Data Protection Law Schleswig-Holstein, and other relevant legal provisions at the State level, and the federal level in the criteria. Also, the data protection by

---

[16] https://www.datenschutzzentrum.de/guetesiegel/register/ (German). Accessed 27 April 2017.

[17] See https://www.datenschutzzentrum.de/guetesiegel/register/. Accessed 27 April 2017.

Fig. 3.2 Distribution of
admitted experts per field
(November 2016) [Source:
M. Hansen]

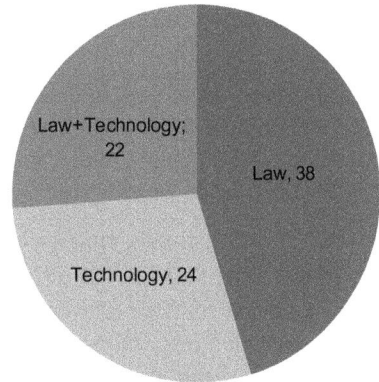

default paradigm (i.e. built-in data protection and privacy-friendly default settings), privacy and data protection goals for privacy engineering,[18] and criteria from the Standard Data Protection Model[19] were added to the catalogue. Input from admitted experts, e.g., collected at annual experts' meetings at the ULD, supports the evolution of the criteria. Further updates will be necessary to reflect the changes arising from European data protection reform.

The number of admitted experts (see Fig. 3.2) has been growing during the evolvement of the Schleswig-Holstein Data Protection Seal because of its increasing visibility. The majority (38 experts; 45%) are admitted legal experts, 24 (29%) are technical experts, and 22 experts including teams working in an evaluation body (26%) have demonstrated combined expertise.[20]

As a spin-off of the *Schleswig-Holstein Data Protection Seal*, the European Privacy Seal (EuroPriSe) was developed. EuroPriSe started as an EU-funded project with the objective of establishing a trans-European privacy seal. Its certification procedure is similar to the *Schleswig-Holstein Data Protection Seal*. Until the end of 2013, the ULD was also the certification body for EuroPriSe. In 2014, the EuroPriSe GmbH was founded; this entity now acts now as the certification body for the scheme. EuroPriSe provides EU-wide privacy certifications that assure compliance with European data protection law. The *Schleswig-Holstein Data Protection Seal* is a partner seal of EuroPriSe; applicants can opt for combined certifications where the evaluation considers both the criteria catalogues.

---

[18] Hansen et al. 2015. See also Sect. 3.5.

[19] The Standard Data Protection Model is an approach for auditing that has been developed in the last years and agreed among all German Data Protection Authorities: https://www.datenschutz-mv.de/datenschutz/sdm/SDM-Methodology_V1_EN1.pdf. Accessed 27 April 2017.

[20] See https://www.datenschutzzentrum.de/guetesiegel/register-sachverstaendige/. Accessed 27 April 2017.

3.5 Lessons Learnt

ULD has been developing and maintaining the *Schleswig-Holstein Data Protection Seal* Programme for about fifteen years and gathered several experiences that helped in the European Privacy Seal initiative, and in reviewing and improving the *Schleswig-Holstein Data Protection Seal*. These are described below:[21]

1. Data protection seals function as trust marks. This requires a **trustworthy and high-quality certification procedure:**

   - **Criteria** must be relevant and facilitate compliance with privacy and data protection legislation.
   - The **evaluation** must be carried out by **experts whose proficiency, reliability and independence is substantiated or demonstrated**. The expert team must comprise **both legal and technical expertise**.
   - Sheer **checkbox approaches usually fall short** in view of complex data processing systems.
   - The **validation** of the evaluation report and the certification in case of approval must be done by an **impartial and knowledgeable certification body, and with due diligence**.
   - For **quality assurance**, evaluation and validation of the evaluation results must be **two distinct steps**. The validation is necessary to check the evaluation report with respect to completeness, plausibility and comparability with other certifications. Our experience shows that in the validation phase it is often necessary to check back with the experts and the applicants, or to have a look at the ToE itself and perform own tests.
   - **Transparency and reliability** of the data protection seal procedure is of utmost importance. This means that information about the procedure itself and the catalogue of criteria should be publicly available. The evaluation report—usually in a summarised form—should be published. The public report should contain the relevant information on the scope of evaluation and the findings. To facilitate comparability, a template for the report should be provided. A specific section of the report should focus on exemplary functionality of the IT product on how it promotes privacy and data protection. This will also be important in the light of the European General Data Protection Regulation[22] Article 25, which calls for data controllers to implement data protection by design and by default.

---

[21] In 2012, an earlier version of this list (compiled by Thomas Probst, ULD, and the author of this text) was used as a contribution to an international discussion on privacy seals within ISO (International Standards Organization).

[22] Regulation (EU) 2016/679 of the European Parliament and of the Council of 27 April 2016 on the protection of natural persons with regard to the processing of personal data and on the free movement of such data, and repealing Directive 95/46/EC (General Data Protection Regulation), Official Journal of the European Union L 119/1 (04.05.2016).

2. In all certification procedures, the **clarity and reasonableness of the ToE** is a pre-requisite:

   - The ToE should be **clearly defined** and agreed on by the applicant, the experts, and the certification body.
   - In case the ToE is only a part of the IT system, its scope should be defined in a way that the ToE is a **substantial part of the IT system as far as privacy and data protection are concerned**.
   - The ToE should be seen as a **coherent product** for potential target users who must not misunderstand the evaluation of the ToE of a part of the IT system as an evaluation of the full IT system. This excludes highly sophisticated definitions of the ToE.
   - It is advisable to reduce complexity of the ToE where possible, e.g., by **dividing the IT system into multiple ToEs** that can evaluated more easily.
   - The ToE always consists not only of the IT product itself, but **all necessary documentation** to understand the product's functionality and to enable potential target users to operate and use it in a way so that privacy and data protection requirements are satisfied. In view of the European General Data Protection Regulation, the documentation should contain the information needed to assess the potential risks e.g. demanded in Articles 24 (Responsibility of the controller), 25 (Data protection by design and by default) and 32 (Security of processing). It should also contain the information needed to conduct a Data Protection Impact Assessment (Article 35).

3. During evaluation, the **technical, organisational and legal framework** within which the ToE is operated (environment) should be taken into account. This includes configuration and settings for relevant components of the IT product, its environment, and organisational and legal aspects such as templates for contracts and (privacy) policies. Note that specialties in jurisdiction or sector-specific law may have to be tackled during the evaluation process.

4. **Privacy and data protection evaluation must not be regarded as a mere "topping" to security evaluation.** From the privacy and data protection perspective, even successful security certifications according to international standards or other proofs of security compliance do not guarantee a stable basis where only some additional issues would have to be checked. Instead, applying privacy and data protection criteria may show a need for a re-conceptualisation and redesign of essential parts of the ToE. The two following examples illustrate this:

   - **Data minimisation and data subjects' rights** are usually not thoroughly checked as part of a security compliance evaluation; often they are not part of the criteria at all. Imagine a ToE that has passed a security evaluation, but relies on the existence of personal data that are not necessary for the purpose: this would defy privacy and data protection principles and legal provisions that demand data minimisation, or the principle of necessity, as contained in European data protection law. Similarly, a successful security evaluation would not help in the case of a ToE not allowing data subjects to exercise their rights that would have to be considered in a privacy and data protection evaluation. Adding this functionality or re-conceptualising and re-designing the ToE would clearly require further security evaluations.

- The security evaluation is usually performed from the perspective of the provider of the ToE. Thus, the perspective of the data subject who may have totally different security requirements is neglected. This effect has been noted already in the discussion on **"multilateral security"**[23] since the 1990s. This concept, first developed in a German inter-disciplinary research group with participation of a variety of universities and a few data protection authorities demands that security requirements of all parties involved in the system should be considered, balanced and agreed upon; all parties should be empowered to enforce the result of that balancing and negotiation process. However, today's system design and operation mostly ignores the principles of multilateral security because the development takes the perspective of the provider and users are not treated at eye level. Although it is possible to supplement evaluation criteria by external requirements which focus on security interests of parties other than the provider of the ToE, this is rarely done. A security evaluation usually does not mitigate the **bias towards providers' interests**. Moreover, privacy and data protection requirements must not be reduced to those (active) participants in the system who can explicitly express their requirements and are able to negotiate with other, usually more powerful stakeholders. Here, privacy and data protection law aims at strengthening the position of the data subjects. This is rarely reflected in present-day security evaluations.

Security evaluations can certainly contribute to the evaluation of technical-organisational measures in a data protection seal procedure. However, they do not guarantee compliance.

5. Many security evaluations are based on the classic triad of the protection goals "confidentiality", "integrity" and "availability". From the data protection perspective, three complementing **privacy and data protection goals** have been introduced: **"unlinkability"** (ensure that privacy-relevant data cannot be linked across privacy domains or used for a different purpose than originally intended), **"transparency"** (ensure that all privacy-relevant data processing including the legal, technical and organisational setting can be understood and reconstructed) and **"intervenability"** (ensure that data subjects, providers and supervisory authorities can intervene in privacy-relevant data processing).[24] All six protection goals are part of the legal framework that drives the criteria of the

---

[23] Rannenberg et al. 1999.

[24] The privacy and data protection goals are part of the Standard Data Protection Model introduced before.

Schleswig-Holstein Data Protection Seal. Since beginning of 2012, the State Data Protection Act Schleswig-Holstein explicitly states that data controllers have to take into account the three IT security protection goals and the three privacy and data protection goals (Article 5 para 1 State Data Protection Act Schleswig-Holstein). With the European General Data Protection Regulation, this approach can and should be continued, especially to ensure data protection by design and by default (Article 25).

6. The **mandatory consideration** of products with a trustworthy data protection seal **in procurement** and in the data protection management system of an organisation should be regulated. While Recital 78 of the European General Data Protection Regulation states that the principles of data protection by design and by default should be taken into consideration in the context of public tenders, additional emphasis is recommended, e.g., by supervisory authorities, or at the level of State or EU administration which should act as a role model.

7. A trustworthy certification process can be expensive. Small companies or **open source initiatives** may not be able to pay for the certification process even if their IT products would meet the requirements. Here, **dedicated funds on Member State or EU level should be established** to support the structured evaluation of data protection and data security criteria of widespread or exemplary IT products during their lifetime. This idea could be implemented by foundations from stakeholders (States, industry, non-governmental organisations, data protection authorities etc.).

3.6   Conclusion

The *Schleswig-Holstein Data Protection Seal* has been a successful endeavour since 2002. The experiences and lessons learnt should be evaluated when setting up new data protection certification schemes in Europe and abroad.

In the implementation of any certification scheme what should be avoided is the reduction in the degree of trustworthiness, e.g., when the certification is not done with due diligence or lacks quality assurance. This would have a negative effect not just on the scheme itself, but also all similar schemes in general.

The Data Protection Authority of Schleswig-Holstein believes that trustworthy data protection seals will play a vital role in the future of data protection in Europe. Therefore, it is evaluating how the concept may need adaption with respect to the European General Data Protection Regulation (GDPR) that will become effective on 25 May 2018. The GDPR contains in Articles 42 and 43 provisions for certifications. In 2016, the Schleswig-Holstein Data Protection Authority initiated the German data protection authority working group on certification for elaborating criteria for accreditation and for certification of the possible groups of Targets of Evaluations. The results of this work as well as the lessons learnt as described in this chapter will be discussed within Germany and on the European level. This encompasses the necessary quality checks of the process (at best in a two-step process), transparent criteria and published short reports as well as the focus on advancing the state-of-the-art of privacy and data protection. There is a plan to continue the certification by the *Schleswig-Holstein Data Protection Seal* scheme in accordance with the provisions from the GDPR, and the upcoming German data protection law.

References

Hansen M, Jensen M, Rost M (2015) Protection Goals for Privacy Engineering. 2015 International Workshop on Privacy Engineering (IWPE), Security and Privacy Workshops (SPW), IEEE, pp 159–166

Hansen M, Probst T (2002) Datenschutzgütesiegel aus technischer Sicht: Bewertungskriterien des schleswig-holsteinischen Datenschutzgütesiegels. In: Bäumler H, von Mutius A (eds) Datenschutz als Wettbewerbsvorteil – Privacy sells: Mit modernen Datenschutz komponenten Erfolg beim Kunden. Vieweg, Wiesbaden, pp 163–179

Rannenberg K, Pfitzmann A, Müller G (1999) IT Security and Multilateral Security. In: Müller G, Rannenberg K (eds) Multilateral Security in Communications – Technology, Infrastructure, Economy. Addison-Wesley-Longman, Massachusetts, pp 21–29

Chapter 4
The French Privacy Seal Scheme:
A Successful Test

(Le schéma français des labels de protection des données: un essai réussi)

Johanna Carvais-Palut

Contents

Abstract With nearly one hundred CNIL privacy seals delivered, France has emerged as a trailblazer in this domain. Realising the importance of changing attitudes and behaviours regarding data protection very early on, the French legislature authorised its supervisory authority to create a new indicator of compliance in this area. The French Data Protection Authority readily admits that its privacy seal is still in the early stages. However, the progress made over the past four years has shown that the experiment was worth pursuing, with a view to creating a lasting scheme. CNIL is now equipped with a proven procedure, elevating its privacy seal to the status of a "guarantee of Ethical Data Protection", in line with CNIL's latest reference standard, the seal on Governance Procedure.

Johanna Carvais-Palut is Data Protection Officer in a French Insurance Company. This chapter was authored in 2016 when Johanna was Head of the Privacy Seals Unit, Compliance Directorate, CNIL [label@cnil.fr].

J. Carvais-Palut (✉)
CNIL, Paris, France
e-mail: label@cnil.fr

© T.M.C. ASSER PRESS and the authors 2018
R. Rodrigues and V. Papakonstantinou (eds.), *Privacy and Data Protection Seals*,
Information Technology and Law Series 28, https://doi.org/10.1007/978-94-6265-228-6_4

Keywords CNIL · governance · accountability · confidence · data protection officer · compliance

4.1 Introduction

With nearly one hundred CNIL[1] privacy seals now delivered, France has emerged as a trailblazer in this domain. Realising the importance of changing attitudes and behaviours regarding data protection very early on, the French legislature authorised its supervisory authority to create a new indicator of compliance in this area. Beyond administrative formalities and the advantages of maintaining a "data protection policing" authority, CNIL privacy seals were borne out of the need to 'responsibilise' organisations in a non-compulsory manner. The 2004 amendment of the French Act of 6 January 1978[2] introduced a provision allowing CNIL to deliver privacy seals for *"products or procedures intended to protect individuals"*.[3]

While the basic premise behind this privacy seal scheme was laid out in theory over ten years ago, it could not be put into practice until the CNIL's internal regulation[4] was amended at the end of 2011.

The French Data Protection Authority readily admits that its privacy seal is still in the early stages. However, the progress made over the past five years has shown that the experiment was worth pursuing, with a view to creating a lasting scheme.

CNIL is now equipped with a proven procedure, elevating its privacy seal to the status of a "guarantee of Ethical Data Protection", in line with CNIL's latest reference standard, which is on Data Protection Governance Procedure.

This chapter looks at the tried and tested CNIL approach, the system underlying the CNIL scheme (Sect. 4.3), the steps in the application process (Sect. 4.4), nature and effect of the CNIL seal (Sect. 4.5), the impact of the scheme and compliance (Sect. 4.6), the 'governance seal' paving the way for the EU Regulation (Sect. 4.7). It concludes with some comments on the future of CNIL seals (Sect. 4.8).

---

[1] Commission Nationale de l'Informatique et des Libertés (CNIL) is the French Data Protection Authority. Created in 1978, CNIL is an Independent Administrative Authority that exercises its functions in accordance with the French Data Protection Act.

[2] French Act 78-17 of 6 January 1978 on Information Technology, Data Files and Civil Liberties (French Data Protection Act).

[3] French Data Protection Act of 1978 amended 6 August 2004.

[4] Decision n° 2011-249 of 8 September 2011 (now amended by Decision n° 2013-175 of 4 July 2013).

4.2   A Tried and Tested System

Rather than issuing a seal certifying compliance with the law, and because *"ignorance of the law is no excuse"*, CNIL instead chose to deliver privacy seals called "Label CNIL"[5] to organisations whose products and procedures are exemplary—a seal that rewards those most deserving and principled, giving them recognition and distinction for going above and beyond what the law requires.

4.3   A Scheme Based on a Two-Phase System

The CNIL scheme is based on a two-phase system.

First, CNIL creates standards listing the requirements to be met and serving as the reference for its compliance analysis. Initially, CNIL could only adopt the standard at the request of a professional organisation. However, the Hamon Act of 17 March 2014[6] provided that the CNIL could also, on its own initiative, determine if a product or procedure is eligible to receive the seal. If initiated by the Commission, this action must correspond to a real need in the sector (based on complaints, CNIL sanctions, or requests from consumer organisations, etc.) and cannot be at the request of a single market player. This new legal framework provides CNIL with greater latitude in choosing its standards. At present, CNIL has

---

[5] www.cnil.fr/en/privacy-seals; www.cnil.fr/fr/les-labels-cnil. Accessed 30 April 2017.

[6] Act 2014-344 of 17 March 2014 (French Consumer Protection Act). The Hamon Act also explicitly introduced into the French Data Protection Act (Article 11-3c) a provision for CNIL to be able to verify that the conditions for receiving the privacy seal are maintained, and to withdraw the privacy seal if necessary.

four reference standards for seals—i.e., data protection training programs,[7] data processing audits,[8] digital safety boxes,[9] and data protection governance.[10]

Second, applicants can—regardless of their affiliation with the organisation that created the standard—apply for a seal based on the four existing standards. The application can be submitted by a single organisation or by several, if the expertise and skills required to receive the seal are distributed between multiple entities, in which case, it is referred to as a "joint application".

Currently, this procedure is managed entirely using CNIL resources, but the French legislature has provided for the possibility of calling on the services of any qualified independent third party to conduct assessments, if the complexity of the

---

[7] Data protection training is a process intended to produce and develop knowledge, know-how and behaviour necessary to compliance with the French data protection act. The said process may take place over several days and include several modules which are independent of each other. The standard defines the criteria and resources enabling the data protection authority to determine whether the training courses for which a privacy seal is requested, achieve such an objective. It includes two parts corresponding to both phases of the evaluation performed by the data protection authority and which cover: the training activity (requirements concerning the method) and the content of the training course (with a main module of fundamental knowledge that the training course must at least include in its curriculum to apply for certification and supplementary modules, that the training course may also include in its curriculum).

[8] A "Data Protection" audit is an audit whose criteria enable judgement of the compliance of processing personal data with the Act No. 78-17 dated 6 January 1978 (French data protection act) amended by the Act No. 2004-801 dated 6 August 2004. The scope of such an audit concerns the processing of personal data implemented within a defined scope, not only in terms of places, organisational units, activities, processes or time periods covered, but also in terms of types of processing or specific processing. The audit procedure describes the conduct, management and content of audits, as they are implemented by the applicant. The complete terminology is presented in the following pages. To this end, the present standard defines the criteria for evaluation relating to the manner of conducting an audit and the processing of personal data during the audit.

[9] The digital safe box, as understood in this standard, covers offers made to individuals concerning services for the dematerialised and secure storage of data, the aim of which is to keep documents on digital media. Digital safe boxes must ensure the integrity, availability and confidentiality of stored data and implement appropriate security measures. A digital safe box is distinguished from an ordinary storage space by the fact that the data retained, including stored documents and their meta data, is accessible only to the holder of the safe box and, where applicable, natural persons whom the holder has specifically authorised for this purpose. The present standard describes the procedures for creation and management, and the content of digital safe boxes. It defines the criteria and the resources allowing the Data Protection Authority to determine whether the digital safe boxes subject to the privacy seal request reach the target objective, namely: the secure retention and protection of personal data contained in a safe box, which will be accessible only to its user and natural persons specifically mandated by the latter.

[10] The governance of personal data protection, also known as "Privacy Governance", establishes the set of measures, rules and best practices that allow for the application of laws and regulations on the handling of personal data as well as provide the specific liabilities inherent to this handling. This privacy seal intends to help private and public organisations implement personal data protection measures and help them be accountable accordingly for their measures. This standard defines the assessment criteria and the means at the Commission's disposal for the assessment of privacy governance procedures' effectiveness in protecting personal data, which is the objective of this privacy seal.

product or procedure justify this measure. This prerogative is costlier than it may seem, because it requires invoicing the applicant for the assessment conducted by the third party, whereas the current CNIL seals have the advantage of being free of charge. At present, French law does not allow CNIL to act as a financial intermediary, i.e., to collect amounts payable to the assessor. Moreover, an assessment conducted by a third party would probably cost several thousand euros (€). French organisations do not yet seem ready to spend such a sizeable sum in this area, although this does appear to be gradually changing.[11]

4.4 A Proven Approach

The privacy seal scheme is voluntary and, to be effective, needs to be fast and clear. Thus, CNIL has developed an application examination procedure in several steps, which takes an average of six months from submission of an application to the delivery of the seal.

The departments are assisted in this task by the Privacy Seal Committee, made up of three of the seventeen CNIL commissioners. The Committee's role is to offer strategic guidelines on the seal deliverance policy. It studies standard drafts and proposals and assesses the compliance of seal applications before they are presented at the CNIL plenary session for approval or refusal.

The various steps in the processing of an application are explained here in detail:[12]

- **The application is submitted** using a form and supplying explanations and evidences. The application can be submitted using an online procedure, by email or by post.
- **The application's admissibility** is determined within two months of its submission. This step involves making sure that the application is officially complete (that the form is duly completed and all appendices are included in full) and ensuring that the product or procedure falls within the scope of the standard in question. If CNIL has not analyzed the application within 2 months, it is deemed admissible.[13]
- **The application is examined by the Privacy Seals Unit**. The compliance assessment can only be carried out after examination of the application by the CNIL "Privacy Seals" centre, which first makes sure that all requirements have been met and reports any areas of non-compliance or points open to interpretation, to the Seal Deliverance Committee. CNIL then has a deliberation period of six months from its receipt of the last piece of additional information required

---

[11] See Sect. 4.6.

[12] Application processing is the second step in the scheme.

[13] See implementation orders for French Act 2000-321 of 12 April 2000 on citizens' rights in their dealings with public bodies (referred to in France as the "DCRA" Act).

to meet all requirements of the standard in question. If no reply is issued within this period, and if the application complies with the standard, it is deemed accepted.[14]

- **The Seal Deliverance Committee assesses the application's compliance.** This Committee meets approximately every three months.
- **The application is then presented at CNIL's plenary session.** This is where the final decision is made as to whether a seal will be delivered or denied.[15]
- **CNIL publishes all decisions** to deliver, renew, or withdraw a seal.[16] However, rejected applications are never published (to encourage submissions). In addition to seal delivery decisions, the names of organisations that have received the seal are published on the CNIL website.[17]

Based on its various reference standards, CNIL delivers a seal for a period of three years, renewable at least six months before the expiration date.[18] At any time throughout the period of validity, CNIL may also verify that the conditions under which the seal was delivered are properly maintained. This may of course be verified by all possible means. A person using a product or procedure that has received the seal can also inform the Commission of any doubt as to its compliance with the reference standard. It could be done by post, or by email. If non-compliance is found, the Commission may decide to withdraw the previously delivered seal after a one-month notice period, during which the organisation may submit its remarks and, if necessary could already take corrective actions.

4.5   A Seal Indicating Proof of Compliance

The EU General Data Protection Regulation (GDPR) refers to the principle of *accountability*,[19] based on the idea that the data controller adopts appropriate rules and takes effective measures to guarantee, and can demonstrate, that personal data are processed in accordance with the Regulation. In its opinion of July 2010,[20] the

---

[14] See Decree 2014-1278 of 23 October 2014.

[15] It could be rejected if CNIL's plenary session considers that the application does not fulfill all the mandatory requirements.

[16] A seal could be withdrawn if the conditions that allowed for the accordance of the privacy seal are no longer fulfilled.

[17] www.cnil.fr. Accessed 30 April 2017.

[18] In August 2016, CNIL delivered 88 seals in total for 110 applications received.

[19] Regulation (EU) 2016/679 of the European Parliament and the Council of 27 April 2016 on the Protection of natural persons with regard to the processing of personal data and on the free movement of such data and repealing Directive 95/46/EC; Article 5.2.

[20] Opinion 3/2010 on the principle of accountability adopted in 13 July 2010 by the Article 29 Data Protection Working Party.

Article 29 Working Party[21] referred to the principle of accountability as contributing to "moving data protection from 'theory to practice.'" The CNIL seal can be viewed as a possible means of implementing this principle. It is even one of the best-suited ways of doing this. After all, what is more reassuring than a privacy seal delivered by a data protection authority to prove one's data protection compliance?

4.6 The CNIL Seal—A Confidence Indicator

Organisations that have received a seal have to submit, in the first year of the grant, an activity report to CNIL. The aim of this report is to verify that the products and procedures granted a seal are in conformity with the standard in question. It also aims to ensure that the "CNIL Privacy Seal" logo is used in compliance with the regulations governing use of the collective mark;[22] and to measure the seal's impact on the organisations that have received it.[23]

The feedback received in these annual activity reports, regarding the benefits of having the seal, has been very positive, generally demonstrating that the organisation sells better (the seal allows it to win tender processes, for example),[24] sells more, and charges higher rates for certified products and services. Thus, the seal improves the company's image. The mark referring to the delivering authority, and its logo in the colours of the French flag, adds to the credibility of the CNIL seal. The high reputation of CNIL clearly has an impact on the seal's ability to create "brand awareness".

When it receives the seal, the recipient undertakes to comply with the standard and, in general, to be exemplary in every aspect of its data processing. This usually involves measures such as implementing an internal privacy policy, conducting audits, setting up procedures, appointing a Data Protection Officer (DPO),[25] and, if applicable, adopting Binding Corporate Rules (BCR). All of this leads to greater awareness, even beyond the issue of data protection, encouraging "corporate social responsibility" based on transparent, and ethical behaviour.

In addition to following the general rules, logo recipients undertake to comply with the Regulations governing use of the collective mark (the "CNIL seal")[26] that they receive along with about twenty different customised logos.[27] These regulations stipulate, for example, that the mark must be used in direct connection with

---

[21] Group of European Data Protection Authorities.

[22] French Regulations governing use of the Collective Mark "CNIL seal" approved by CNIL on 14 June 2012.

[23] Such as a better acknowledgment of the expertise in the industry.

[24] As the seal is increasingly being well-recognised, a lot of tender procurement policies for data protection trainings or audits now require the CNIL seal.

[25] In France, we have an equivalent called a "Correspondant Informatique et Libertés (CIL)".

[26] French Regulations governing use of the Collective Mark "CNIL seal" approved by CNIL on 14 June 2012.

[27] Different sizes and different colors (blue, white and red or black and white) for several uses.

the product or procedure that has received the seal. The Regulations strictly prohibit making general use of the seal or displaying it indiscriminately. The Regulations also set out the limitations on use of the registered mark, e.g., that the recipient must agree not to use the mark for political purposes, or in ways that are controversial, or contrary to public interest or accepted principles of morality.

The Regulations also require the recipient to maintain strict conduct corresponding to the consumer's perception of the seal as a mark of quality and reliability.

4.7 The "Governance" Seal, Paving the Way for the EU Regulation

Privacy governance has been a major focus for CNIL over the past several years. Since 2011, the Commission has contributed to the drafting of standards on privacy management systems which were elaborated by the International Organization for Standardization (ISO). CNIL is also studying the development of tools to help those following its recommendations to fully benefit from them.

Until 2014, CNIL could only deliver seals at the request of professionals,[28] but the French legislature has since granted the Commission the right to act on its own initiative. For CNIL, this offers new opportunity in terms of what it can achieve with its "governance" standard, i.e.:

- using the privacy seal as a tool to build accountability;
- starting to inform companies about the EU General Data Protection Regulation and working on changing attitudes within French companies;
- providing an instruction manual for beginner DPOs and providing support for experienced DPOs (for whom receiving the seal may be a goal);
- focusing attention on small and medium enterprises (SMEs)[29] that do not fit the profile for a seal, and large groups that already have BCR to help them obtain the seal more easily.

Developing the standard on Data Protection Governance, CNIL asked three French associations for their opinions on the relevance of content. Two chose to give their point of view, one of which conducted a survey among its members. The survey[30] showed that 72% of the respondents thought their organisation would be interested in obtaining the seal, or that they would do their utmost to encourage the organisation to get the seal.[31]

Based on these findings, all agreed to target organisations from every sector (companies, municipalities, associations, public establishments, universities, etc.),

---

[28] Ibid.

[29] Small and Medium-sized Enterprises.

[30] Seventy-six people completed the survey. It was launched between September and November 2014.

[31] Note: 20% of the respondents did not answer this question.

if they had a DPO. The standard on Privacy Governance has, in its latest version, twenty-five cumulative requirements, which are divided into three parts:

- **the internal organisation relating to data protection** (with requirements for the data protection policy and its status, training, resources, and the DPO's activities);
- **the method for verifying data processing compliance with the French Data Protection Act**[32] (with requirements on analysis and compliance investigations);
- **the handling of claims and incidents** (with requirements on the handling of claims and rights of individuals, the documentation of security incidents, and the handling of data breaches).

Thanks to the initial enthusiasm from the associations, organisations in both public and private sectors have received the seal, starting with the year the standard was adopted. All of this bodes well for application of the EU Regulation. It appears that French organisations are gradually preparing themselves to meet their obligations under the GDPR.[33]

4.8   What Lies Ahead for CNIL Seals?

In light of the EU General Data Protection Regulation (GDPR), which encourages the adoption of data protection certifications, seals and marks,[34] the French privacy seal scheme developed by CNIL is destined not only to be sustainable, but to diversify, e.g., with the launch of other schemes (e.g., scheme to accredit third-party certification bodies). CNIL will also work with the European Data Protection Board[35] to create a European Privacy seal.

---

[32] French Act 78-17 of 6 January 1978 on Information Technology, Data Files and Civil Liberties (French Data Protection Act).

[33] Regulation (EU) 2016/679 of the European Parliament and the Council of 27 April 2016 on the Protection of natural persons with regard to the processing of personal data and on the free movement of such data and repealing Directive 95/46/EC.

[34] Article 42 and Recital 100 of the Regulation (EU) 2016/679 of the European Parliament and the Council of 27 April 2016 on the Protection of natural persons with regard to the processing of personal data and on the free movement of such data and repealing Directive 95/46/EC.

[35] The European Data Protection Board will be set up as an independent body of the Union with legal personality. It will replace the Article 29 Working Party on the Protection of Individuals with regard to the Processing of Personal Data established by Directive 95/46/EC. It will consist of the head of a supervisory authority of each Member State and the European Data Protection Supervisor or their respective representatives. The Board will contribute to the consistent application of the GDPR throughout the Union, including by advising the Commission, in particular on the level of protection in third countries or international organisations, and promoting cooperation of the supervisory authorities throughout the Union.

CNIL intends to pursue its privacy seal deliverance and compliance tool development policy. It will also encourage the publication of new European standards, for without question, therein lies the most difficult challenge, and the most awaited step forward.

CNIL ventured early into the domain of privacy compliance. Four years later, with almost eighty privacy seals delivered, the test seems to be a success.

Chapter 5
Privacy Seals in the USA, Europe, Japan, Canada, India and Australia

Ann Cavoukian and Michelle Chibba

Contents

Abstract The concept of having a visual identifier has evolved over time from a relatively simple mark, such as a hallmark, essentially informing a consumer of the purity of a substance to certifying products coming from an enormously complex system such as food or pharmaceuticals. There have been several initiatives in

A. Cavoukian (✉) · M. Chibba
Privacy by Design Centre of Excellence, Ryerson University, Toronto, Canada
e-mail: ann.cavoukian@ryerson.ca

M. Chibba
e-mail: michelle.chibba@ryerson.ca

© T.M.C. ASSER PRESS and the authors 2018   59
R. Rodrigues and V. Papakonstantinou (eds.), *Privacy and Data Protection Seals*,
Information Technology and Law Series 28, https://doi.org/10.1007/978-94-6265-228-6_5

different jurisdictions to have this same external validation of privacy and data protection integrity through certification, seals of approval, or trust marks. A wide range of approaches have been initiated in several jurisdictions around the world, each with specific requirements and results. This chapter provides a scan of the USA, Europe, Japan, Canada, India and Australia with a focus on selected certification, seal or trust mark programs for online privacy and data protection. It compiles publicly available information on the current features of the program behind the icon, background on the lead organisation or trust mark provider, any details of historical significance particularly for the schemes that have in place for over ten years, as well as some general observations.

Keywords privacy seal · privacy certification · privacy trust mark · data protection · consumer protection · e-commerce

5.1 Introduction

By way of background and historical context, stamps, seals, certifications or marks (as they have been called) have existed in other sectors for centuries. As far back as the fourteenth century, England established the hallmark, known as one of the oldest forms of protection for consumers. A hallmark is simply a stamp, impressed upon articles of precious metal certifying the percentage of metal content—yet the significance of such a mark was far greater. How else could a consumer possibly know what they were buying without some validation or assurance? Eventually, merchants recognised the value of having a hallmark to attest to one's reputation and adherence to industry standards. With the introduction of the hallmark, the competitive advantage shifted from fraudulent manipulators to a reputation for quality assurance.[1]

The concept of having a visual identifier continued to evolve over time from a relatively simple mark, essentially informing the buyer of the purity of a substance to certifying products coming from an enormously complex system such as food or pharmaceuticals. This tradition continues to be relevant when examining the privacy seals marketplace. In other words, a privacy trust mark serves as a logical corollary that a specific privacy code or standard had been successfully met. Moreover, it informs consumers, in a simple and powerful way that an item or service is being marketed within a system of verified accountability and responsibility—in this case, pertaining to online privacy and data protection.

---

[1] Newman undated.

There have been several initiatives in different jurisdictions to have external validation of privacy and data protection integrity through certification, seals of approval or trust marks.[2] A wide range of approaches have been established, each with specific requirements and results. This chapter provides a scan of the USA, Europe, Japan, Canada, India and Australia with a focus on selected certification, seal or trust mark programs for online privacy and data protection. It does not evaluate the effectiveness of the scheme but rather compiles publicly available information on the current features of the program being offered, background on the lead organisation and any details of historical significance particularly for the schemes that have in place for over 15 years. In some cases, we can build upon, update and supplement earlier work on privacy seal inventories and comparative analysis. We also provide some general observations based on the research and comparative analysis.

5.2 Comparative Analysis

5.2.1 Government Interest in Online Privacy Seal as a Self-Regulatory and Consumer Awareness Mechanism

In our research, we found that privacy certification, seals and trust marks have been studied extensively by governments, researchers and industry self-regulatory organisations. The impetus for governments, for the most part, related to the desire to ride the wave of e-commerce but at the same time acknowledging the significance of consumer trust in such an evolution. Privacy seals was one of several mechanisms examined to enhance consumer online privacy. The European Commission published an extensive inventory and analysis of privacy certification schemes[3] to identify procedures and mechanisms necessary for the successful launch of a European-wide certification scheme, (e.g., EU privacy seals) regarding the privacy compliance of processes, technologies, products and services.

There has been some minimal overlap between government regulation of privacy and trust mark schemes, although to date this has been restricted to a few instances in the United States. For example, several trust mark schemes, including TRUSTe, are approved complaints resolution bodies for the purposes of the EU Safe Harbour regime. Their actual legal role in the Safe harbour regime is limited to the provision

---

[2] In this chapter, we use the terms certification, seal and trust mark interchangeably.

[3] Rodrigues et al. 2013.

of dispute resolution services. Similarly, a small number of trust mark schemes, including TRUSTe, kidSAFE and Privo, have been approved by the Federal Trade Commission (FTC) as complaints resolution bodies for the purposes of the Children's Online Privacy Protection Act and related Rule (COPPA).

In November 2011, the Asia-Pacific Economic Cooperation (APEC) leaders issued a directive to implement its Cross Border Privacy Rules System (CBPR). The CBPR system balances the flow of information and data across borders while at the same time providing effective protection for personal information. The system is one by which the privacy policies and practices of companies operating in the APEC region are assessed and certified by a third-party verifier (known as an "Accountability Agent") and follows a set of commonly-agreed upon rules, based on the APEC Privacy Framework. As of early 2016, four APEC economies— Japan, Mexico, Canada, and the United States—have aligned their privacy laws with the APEC Privacy Framework.

CBPR Accountability Agents are any organisation that does one or both of two things: certifies the compliance of business developed CBPRs with the APEC framework; and provides an efficient dispute resolution service to provide an avenue for consumers to address privacy complaints with business. While an accountability agent may be a government agency or regulator, such as a privacy commissioner, the term also includes privacy trust marks. An accountability agent is responsible for both review of applications for CBPR and for enforcement if there are questions about compliance. On the CBPR website, JIPDEC[4] and TRUSTe are named as approved accountability agents.[5]

The 2016 European General Data Protection Regulation (GDPR) states that, "In order to enhance transparency and compliance with this Regulation, the establishment of certification mechanisms and data protection seals and marks should be encouraged, allowing data subjects to quickly assess the level of data protection of relevant products and services."[6]

5.2.2 Unregulated Trust Mark Sector Leads to Wide Range of Privacy Trust Mark Providers

Self-regulatory instruments in the private sector involve a number of policy instruments such as privacy commitments, privacy codes, privacy standards and privacy seals.[7] One view of the trust mark sector was that it is completely

---

[4] https://english.jipdec.or.jp/Aboutus.html. Accessed 1 May 2017.

[5] See http://www.cbprs.org/. APEC Cross Border Privacy Rules (CBPR) system. Accessed 1 June 2016.

[6] Regulation (EU) 2016/679 of The European Parliament and of the Council of 27 April 2016.

[7] Bennett 2004.

unregulated and any organization could run a trust mark service.[8] At that time, trust mark associations were rare, an example being the Asia-Pacific Trustmark Alliance (APTA), which was established in 2003 as a regional alliance.[9] The sheer number of privacy seals listed in the EU Report inventory,[10] despite narrowing the scope of the search, is a reflection of this open market.

Several of the comparative reports on privacy seals enumerated categories of trust mark providers such as: industry organisations made up of private for- and non-profit member organisations; accrediting authorities who are created or led by government institutions; private organisations that are single, private for- or non-profit entities who oversee a trust mark and; those that are not distinctly private or public.

In our scan of these reports, we found that the report would, for the most part, capture a point in time of a particular privacy seal program. We found that over time, a program may evolve in terms of its governance structure generally crossing from non-profit to profit or public to private (e.g., EuroPriSe, TRUSTe).

5.2.3   Privacy Trust Mark Programs Are Continuously Evolving

Privacy certification and seals took off in the late 1990s as a means to generate consumer trust and confidence in online business. It is no wonder then, that the subject of Web privacy seals was raised in September 1999 at the 21st Conference of International Data Protection Commissioners. It was felt that a preliminary assessment of the major Web seal programs would be a useful contribution to the global debate over online privacy. The Web seal project evaluated the three leading online privacy seals at that time: BBBOnLine, TRUSTe and WebTrust, all US based but reflecting different models. The project identified three key components for an effective online seal program: sufficient privacy principles to which participating Web sites must adhere; a sound method for resolving disputes between consumers and Web sites; and a robust mechanism for ensuring that "sealed" Web sites complied with the seal's standards.[11]

One of the conclusions in the Web seal project was that "One current limitation with some seals is that, at this stage at least, they formally cover only the

---

[8] Connolly 2008.

[9] In 2010, the APTA broadened its horizons beyond the region to become a global alliance and was renamed the World Trustmark Alliance (WTA) in 2010. Although membership is primarily from the Asia-Pacific region, there are some US and European trust mark members. Of the schemes included in this chapter, only TRUSTe is identified as a member.

[10] Rodrigues et al. 2013.

[11] Cavoukian and Crompton 2000.

Web-based component of business-to-consumer transactions. They do not cover other elements of that relationship."[12]

The EU study of privacy seal programs found that "From 2011 onwards, privacy and data protection certification schemes aiming at a niche or specialised segment of the market start to emerge more prominently. This may be a sign that the certification schemes market is segmenting from a broader approach to a more targeted approach, that there are increasingly specific sets of privacy or information processing concerns, or that certification scheme operators see a potential gap and market for such schemes as opposed to general trust mark schemes."[13] The recent initiative to introduce a TrustMark for Biometrics out of the Biometrics Institute in Australia is a good example. Although the US ESRB Privacy Certified seals are for the video and gaming industry and for a specific market, it is one of the longer standing privacy seal program.

Instead of passive and somewhat cumbersome approaches such as lists of approved organisations on a Trust Mark provider's website, embedding capabilities into the actual trust mark is more user friendly. For example, the icon or seal may include details of the validity, registration and to confirm that it is an active registration by also embedding a link back to the provider for confirmation.

Since e-commerce is rapidly changing with technology and consumer preferences, privacy seal programs must also adapt to remain relevant and of value to consumer privacy and data protection. Indeed, in their evaluation, the Privacy Commissioners acknowledged the potential for privacy seal programs to evolve.[14]

5.2.4 Transparency Is Becoming a Trust Mark Provider Differentiator

Transparency has always been an essential component of accountability. In fact, the Article 29 Working Party in their report on accountability notes "As certain seals become known for their rigorous testing, data controllers are likely to favour them insofar as they would give more compliance 'comfort' in addition to offering a competitive advantage."[15] By extension, to be meaningful, a certification or seal will depend heavily upon the scope of the certification process and the roles of the actors involved. To determine this, however, whether it is a regulator, the government as policy maker, the researcher engaged in comparative analysis and evaluation, a client/potential member seeking to participate in a trust mark program, or a consumer, at a minimum and as starting point, information about the program needs to be publicly available, easy to locate and understand.

---

[12] Ibid.

[13] Rodrigues et al. 2013.

[14] Cavoukian and Crompton 2000.

[15] Article 29 Data Protection Working Party 2010.

Here, we turn to the EU report authors' description of the 'limitations and problems' encountered while trying to find information on some of the privacy seal programs required for their inventory. We found similar challenges in conducting our scan for this chapter. For the most part, there was the lack of availability and accessibility to information as well as limitations on the depth and quality of the information provided. Our scan was also limited due to language barriers.

It is no wonder then, that an earlier report on privacy seal schemes notes that after more than 10 years of operation, the actual level of privacy protection provided by a trust mark was still poorly understood by consumers.[16] Trust marks can easily be faked and software is available online to recreate them. One way to confirm the authenticity of a trust mark is if the issuer publishes current and valid organisations on a publicly available website. Many issues have designed their logos with a hyperlink for convenience and ease of accountability. If there is no mechanism for the public to confirm an organisation's certification status and the number of fraudulent or expired certifications are allowed to proliferate, trust and confidence in the mechanism will diminish.

The privacy seal, trust mark programs that we outline below reflect those where information was readily available either through the website, third party reports, or through direct communication with the provider.

5.3 The United States

In 1999, the US Federal Trade Commission (FTC) revisited[17] their earlier findings that expressed concerns about the progress of industry self-regulation to protect consumers' privacy on the Internet as well as specific concerns about protecting children's privacy online.[18] In its report to Congress, the FTC included an examination of privacy seal programs as one of "several significant and promising self-regulatory programs....underway".[19] However, the report also noted that, at that time, it was too early to assess the effectiveness of the programs (e.g., TRUSTe, BBBOnLine Privacy Seal, ESRB Privacy Online, CPA WebTrust) in serving as a mechanism to protect consumers' online privacy. Many of the other early reports on privacy seals also focussed on TRUSTe, BBBOnline, ESRB and WebTrust, all early US based initiatives.

Several other seals that originated in the US also exist on the Internet. For example, there is the VeriSign program, which is mostly for security through encryption and authentication products, or the International Computer Security Association's (ICSA) seal. Other US initiatives available internationally include:

---

[16] Connolly 2008.

[17] FTC 1999.

[18] The US Congress passed the Children's Online Privacy Protection Act of 1998 (COPPA).

[19] FTC 1999.

Cloud Security Alliance, Transaction Guard, Gigya, McAfee Secure. Those that are offered domestically include buySafe, PRIVO, iKeepSafe, smartgrid privacy seal.[20] For this chapter, the authors provide an overview of the international ESRB, TRUSTe and an update on BBBOnline. WebTrust is covered in the Canadian section (see Sect. 5.6) of this chapter.

5.3.1 ESRB Privacy Certified Program Seals

Located in New York City, the Entertainment Software Rating Board (ESRB)[21] is an example of a US based privacy seal program that is offered through an industry association. ESRB is a non-profit, self-regulatory body established in 1994 by the Entertainment Software Association (ESA) that assigns ratings for video games and apps. The ESRB rating system encompasses guidance about age-appropriateness, content, and interactive elements. As part of its self-regulatory role for the video game industry, the ESRB also helps ensure responsible online and mobile privacy practices among member companies participating in its Privacy Certified program.

According to its website, ESRB Privacy Certified is a full-service online privacy program that was launched in 1999 and expanded to mobile app services in 2013. The program provides ongoing monitoring and consulting services designed to identify potential issues on an ongoing basis and works with members to address the issues. The purpose of the services under ESRB Privacy Certified is to help members maintain compliance with privacy laws and established best practices in the United States and Canada, European Union (EU), Asia-Pacific region and South America. In 2012, ESRB formed a strategic partnership, offering Veratad's online verification solutions in conjunction with the privacy seal and certification services of the ESRB Privacy Online program.

Three different seals are offered, see Fig. 5.1. The "ESRB Privacy Certified" seal signifies that a general audience website complies with global privacy laws and best practices. The "Kids Online Privacy Compliance Seal" signifies that a child-directed website or app complies with applicable laws and requirements such as COPPA in the US. The "ESRB Privacy Certified for Mobile" seal signifies that a mobile app complies with mobile privacy standards and best practices.

The ESRB Privacy Certified website claims that it supports over 2,000 member websites and apps. To verify membership, members post a "Click to Confirm" badge on their Privacy Policy page, which certifies that the company is a member of the ESRB Privacy Certified program in good standing. ESRB also offers potential members an online Privacy Risk Assessment, which it says will help inform a discussion about possible ESRB assistance. Once an eligible organisation joins the program, ESRB says that it will work with the organisation to implement the

---

[20] Rodrigues et al. 2013.
[21] https://www.esrb.org/privacy/. Accessed 1 June 2016.

Fig. 5.1 ESRB Privacy Mark
[Source: ESRB Privacy
Certified Member Services.
http://www.esrb.org/privacy/
member_services.aspx.
Accessed 17 December 2017]

necessary changes, after which the sites and/or apps will be certified along with approval to display the applicable ESRB Privacy Certified seals.

ESRB Privacy Certified indicates that it conducts two reviews each year for every website it certifies and randomly checks members' mobile apps to ensure their published privacy policy is accurate and up-to-date. Regularly conducted spot checks are also conducted to identify areas for improvement. These checks involve ESRB staff posing as a user to assess how the website or app collects and uses its users' personal information. ESRB offers a Consumer Online Hotline that is always available to consumers who have not satisfactorily resolved a privacy issue with a member company.

The fee for any of the seals is included in the membership fees. Membership fees for the ESRB Privacy Certified program are on a sliding scale based on a company's annual revenue (starting at $0).

5.3.2 TRUSTe

TRUSTe[22] was founded in 1997 by the Electronic Frontier Foundation and the CommerceNet Consortium[23] as an independent non-profit industry association with a mission of fostering online commerce by helping businesses and other online organisations self-regulate privacy concerns. TRUSTe started out with website privacy certification and grew along the way to introduce more products and services as part of its 'seal' program. On 15 July 2008 TRUSTe changed its status from non-profit to for-profit and accepted investment from Accel—part-owners of Facebook.[24]

Based on its website, TRUSTe provides data privacy management solutions and services, including assessments, certifications and its SaaS-based platform. TRUSTe is a widely recognised Internet seal program, with nearly 2,000 Web sites displaying the TRUSTe seal. See Fig. 5.2. To verify if a site is TRUSTe Certified, the TRUSTe Seal on the website links to an active TRUSTe Validation Page hosted on truste.com. TRUSTe also hosts a Trusted Directory to determine if a site is TRUSTe Certified. TRUSTe's Feedback and Resolution System is available to address concerns or an unresolved privacy dispute with a participant in a TRUSTe

---

[22] https://www.truste.com/. Accessed 1 June 2016.

[23] Rifon et al. 2005.

[24] Connolly 2008.

Fig. 5.2 Truste Seal [Source:
TRUSTe Privacy Certification
Seal. https://www.trustarc.
com/products/enterprise-
privacy-certification/.
Accessed 17 December 2017]

TRUSTe

certification program. TRUSTe also provides a link to report potential trademark violations.

TRUSTe certifies against a wide range of privacy standards i.e., EU-US Privacy Shield Customer and HR Data, Model Contract Clauses, APEC, COPPA, Fair Information Practice Principles (FIPPs), Generally Accepted Privacy Principles, (GAPP), Organisation for Economic Co-operation and Development (OECD), California Online Privacy Protection Act (CalOPPA), European Interactive Digital Advertising Alliance (EDAA). TRUSTe notes that it has a team of 150+ privacy professionals dedicated to providing a full range of services to meet privacy compliance for a wide range of products and services such as: websites, mobile apps, and cloud platforms; online and offline data sources; customer, partner, and employee/human resource data sources; cross border data transfers; data processor and data controller relationships.

Successful organisations must recertify annually and there are also provisions to terminate or suspend an organisation's participation in the program.

5.3.3 Better Business Bureau (BBB) Online

In March 1999, the Council of Better Business Bureaus (CBBB) released a privacy seal program called BBBOnline. Three seals were available under the program. One on reliability, one for privacy and one specific to children.[25] CBBB,[26] a non-profit self-regulatory organisation, has a mutually-supportive relationship with National Partners or Better Business Bureaus (BBB) in the United States, Canada and Mexico, which serve accredited BBB businesses and consumers in their local communities. The BBB Online Privacy Seal service stopped taking new applications in 2007 and the complete service (including managing complaints for existing accredited sites) ceased on 1 July 2008.[48] Many sites still display the seal. BBB Online does provide a generic Reliability Seal. However, the privacy standards

---

[25] Bennett 2004.

[26] See more at: http://www.bbb.org/council/about/council-of-better-business-bureaus/#sthash. ICFRxhee.dpuf. Accessed 1 June 2016.

required under this service are significantly lower than those required under the former online privacy seal program.[27]

Information on the website emphasises that BBB accreditation[28] does not mean that the business's products or services have been evaluated or endorsed by BBB, or that BBB has made a determination as to the business' product quality or competency in performing services. Businesses are under no obligation to seek BBB accreditation, and some businesses are not accredited because they have not sought BBB accreditation.

BBB Code of Business Practices, to which businesses are accredited, are built on the BBB Standards for Trust, eight principles that summarise important elements of creating and maintaining trust in business. Among the elements such as "Build Trust" "Advertise Honestly" "Tell the Truth" "Be Transparent" "Honor Promises" "Be Responsive", "Embody Integrity" is "Safeguard Privacy"—protect any data collected against mishandling and fraud, collect personal information only as needed, and respect the preferences of consumers regarding the use of their information.

5.4   Europe

There is significant diversity among existing trust marks in the EU. Some points of distinction are: a formal accreditation of a trust mark, the nature of organisations which administer trust marks, their sources of funding, involvement of stakeholders, geographical and substantive scope of coverage, monitoring traders' compliance and sanctioning non-compliance. Issue areas covered by an earlier discussion of requirements for a Pan-European trust mark that were meant to form a basis for good online practices were identified as: high standard, measurability and purpose of trust mark schemes; transparency of trust mark schemes for consumers and businesses; accessibility and visibility of trust mark schemes for consumers and businesses; scope and content of trust mark schemes.[29]

In Europe, e-commerce and a Digital Single Market continue to be priorities and concerns about consumers' lack of trust as one of the barriers hampering the development of online businesses selling goods and/or services cross-border. This appears to be the impetus for a more global approach to a privacy seal or trust mark. Moreover, the recent introduction of the General Data Protection Regulation (GDPR) in 2016 will have significant implications for certification practices and initiatives. Herein, we provide an overview of EuroPriSe, and European eCommerce and Omni-Channel Trade Association (EMOTA) European TrustMark.

---

[27] Connolly 2008.

[28] See more at: http://www.bbb.org/lexington/for-businesses/about-bbb-accreditation/#sthash.cKnUU4X3.dpuf. Accessed 1 June 2016.

[29] Directorate-General for Internal Policies 2012.

5.4.1 EuroPriSe

EuroPriSe began in 2003 as an EU funded project with a view to establishing a trans-European privacy seal operated through the German data protection authority the Independent Centre for Privacy Protection Schleswig-Holstein (ULD). The program was formally launched in 2009 after two years of development by an international consortium the European Union. EuroPriSe is short for the European Privacy Seal, which is given to individual products and services that fulfill an assessment of legal and technical compliance with European data protection laws.

In November 2013, ULD announced that it was transferring operations to a new entity to be known as EuroPriSe GmbH as of 1 January 2014. The purpose was to allow the program to grow in a way that was not possible as part of a regulatory body like ULD. Instead, ULD would continue to serve as part of its advisory board. The hope, said van Staden, is that the seal will have value globally, in "that it came right from Euro regulations, and it's something companies can use to show compliance with European regulation, that they're doing everything they can to comply."[30]

Based on its website, EuroPriSe offers certifications for IT products and IT-based services throughout the EU. IT products that comply with EU data protection law. Some examples include, but are not limited to, mobile devices, medical devices, computer applications or smart entertainment systems. EuroPriSe certifies services that use IT to collect and process data that conform to EU data protection law. Some examples include, but are not limited to, Software as a Service (SaaS), IT maintenance services, or HR services.

As of 2015, EuroPriSe certifies websites that comply with EU data protection law. This includes websites from many different fields and is not limited to those of IT products and IT-based services. The EuroPriSe seal can also be awarded to businesses that are commissioned to process data for a third party. Some examples of this include, but are not limited to, email marketing services or online storage services. EuroPriSe offers applicants the possibility to conduct combined certification projects together with ULD, the Office of the Data Protection Commissioner of Schleswig-Holstein, Germany. ULD certifies compliance of hardware, software, automated procedures and services with German/Schleswig-Holstein data protection law. Successful finalisation of a combined certification project results in the award of both, the European Privacy Seal (see Fig. 5.3 and the ULD-Gütesiegel).

A EuroPriSe seal assures users that their personal data are handled in accordance with European data protection laws[31] and offers to guarantee transparency, a legal basis for processing personal and sensitive personal data, compliance with data protection principles and duties, technical-organisational measures, data subject rights under Directive 95/46/EC and Directive 2002/58/EC.[32]

---

[30] https://iapp.org/news/a/europrise-seal-to-change-hands-january-11. Accessed 1 June 2016.

[31] https://www.european-privacy-seal.eu/EPS-en/Home. Accessed 1 June 2016.

[32] Rodrigues et al. 2013.

Fig. 5.3 European Privacy Seal [Source: European Privacy Seal Fact Sheet. https://www.european-privacy-seal.eu/EPS-en/fact-sheet. Accessed 17 December 2017]

The EuroPriSe Advisory Board meets twice per year and provides opinions on the following matters: changes to existing inspection schemes (particularly, the EuroPriSe Criteria Catalogue); new certification products (e.g., website certification or commissioned data processing certification); disputes between EuroPriSe CA and EuroPriSe Experts regarding legal or technical issues of general importance and; matters raised by EuroPriSe experts which are presented to the board by the experts' representative.

The certification process involves the following: the organisation chooses a legal and a technical expert from the expert register and discusses the evaluation with the experts; then the organisation meets with the certification authority and agrees on the evaluation with the experts; the next step is to apply for certification and conclude a Certification Agreement with the Certification Authority; the experts conduct the evaluation and complete an evaluation report as approved by the organization to submit to the Certification Authority; a brief report to be made public is also compiled by the experts and approved by the organization. The EuroPriSe certification fees are not publicly available on the website but are available upon request.

The privacy certificate aims to facilitate an increase of market transparency for privacy relevant products and growth in the demand for Privacy Enhancing Technologies (PETs) and finally an increase of trust in IT. EuroPriSe offers its privacy certification to IT products, IT-based services and websites that are compliant with EU data protection regulations. EuroPriSe also certifies commissioned data processing, participates in combined certification projects with the German ULD-Gütesiegel and is qualified to award the German Gutesiegel (M-V).

5.4.2 EMOTA European Trustmark

The European eCommerce and Omni Channel Trade Association (EMOTA), is the European federation representing Online and Omni Channel trade across Europe. The mission of EMOTA is to promote ecommerce and advocate for removal of trade barriers. EMOTA is active in promoting best practices for webshops. EMOTA has its office in Brussels and members are: Handelsverband (Austria), Safeshops.be

Fig. 5.4 EMOTA Trust
Mark [Source: EMOTA
European Trustmark for
e-commerce. https://www.
emota.eu/european-trustmark.
Accessed 17 December 2017]

(Belgium), ASML (Finland), bvh (Germany), Bundesverband der Deutschen Versandbuchhändler (also Germany), EPAM (Greece), ACSEL (France), Magyar Áruküldök Egyesülete (Hungary), Netcomm (Italy), Acepi (Portugal), Allegro Group (also Portugal) and Namo (Russia).

EMOTA launched its European trustmark for online merchants, March 2014.[33] The EMOTA European Trustmark[34] allows consumers to find reliable and trustworthy merchants selling online. This is not a specific privacy trustmark, but rather includes privacy and data protection as one of the quality standards for consumers when making online purchases. The EMOTA European Trustmark is operated by the national certification bodies that are accredited by the EMOTA Trustmark Board. To apply for the Trustmark, an applicant should directly contact its national Trustmark provider.

The association, which claims to represent more than 80% of the ecommerce industry in Europe, establishes harmonised certificate criteria for all national trust marks in Europe. EMOTA's goal is to improve the customers' confidence in online shopping across border, and increase the cross-border turnover for European online stores. The European trust mark should also overcome the language barriers of national trust marks. "Compliance with our criteria will be monitored and traders not acting in conformity with the codes of conduct of our accredited trust marks will lose the benefit of displaying our European label on their websites", said Susanne Czech, Secretary General of EMOTA.

The EMOTA Trust mark (see Fig. 5.4) is a co-branded model.[35] The EMOTA European e-Commerce Trustmark cannot be displayed as a stand-alone trust mark. It can only be displayed together with an accredited national e-Commerce trust mark. At the time of writing of this chapter, EMOTA had 12 European partner countries.

EMOTA's accreditation process includes: documented procedure to ensures merchants' compliance with the trust mark requirements; support and advice to implement improvements before the trust mark can be awarded; record of accreditation based on approved terms & conditions; continuous monitoring of

---

[33] http://ecommercenews.eu/emota-launches-european-trustmark-for-ecommerce/. Accessed 1 June 2016.

[34] http://www.emota.eu/#!european-trustmark-/c1f52. Accessed 1 June 2016.

[35] Presentation by EMOTA Secretary General 2014.

traders' compliance based on a minimum annual review including random checks; alternative dispute resolution (ADR) resources to assist with consumer complaints; and finally, enforcement and sanctions where merchants need to correct any issues promptly that could lead to withdrawal of the Trustmark if found in non-compliance with the code of conduct.

EMOTA will coordinate the accreditation and dispute resolution processes by leveraging external resources (e.g., ombudsman/law firm compliance check of national trust marks' codes of conduct with EU level criteria).

5.5 Japan—PrivacyMark

The impetus for establishing a privacy seal or mark in Japan was based on the view that for online businesses and services to grow, both companies and individuals would require a secure environment in which privacy was a predominant feature. With such foresight, the Japan Information Processing Development Center (JIPDEC) established, and has been operating the PrivacyMark program[36] since 1 April 1998.

JIPDEC was established as a non-profit organisation in 1967 with support from then Ministry of International Trade and Industry (MITI), Ministry of Posts and Telecommunications (MPT) and the private sector. JIPDEC's mission is to promote Japan's IT industry. In May 1988, JIPDEC published "Guidelines for personal data protection in the private sector" because of increased online privacy concerns. Since April 2005, the "Act on the Protection of Personal Information" [Japan Law No. 57, 2003] referred to as the Personal Information Protection Law, has been fully enforced in Japan. Shortly thereafter, on 27 June 2005, JIPDEC was authorised by the Minister for Economy, Trade and Industry (METI) and the Minister for Internal Affairs and Communications (MIAC) as an Authorized Personal Information Protection Organization pursuant to Clause 1, Article 37 of the Act. Since June 2008, JIPDEC established a mutual recognition program with Dalian Software Industry Association (DSIA) in China. On 1 April 2011, JIPDEC became a general incorporated foundation with a Board of Directors.

Japan's PrivacyMark system (see Fig. 5.5) aims to guarantee appropriate protective measures for personal information. This system evaluates the handling of private information by a business in a fair and neutral manner, from a third-party standpoint. The system follows the Japanese Industry Standard "Personal information protection management system—Requirements" (JIS Q 15001) which establishes a rigorous set of rules and procedures for the securing of personal information. Based on eligibility and qualifications, businesses that meet the requirements of these rules and procedures may use the PrivacyMark logo. As of

---

[36] http://privacymark.org/privacy_mark/about/outline_and_purpose.html#section1. Accessed 1 June 2016.

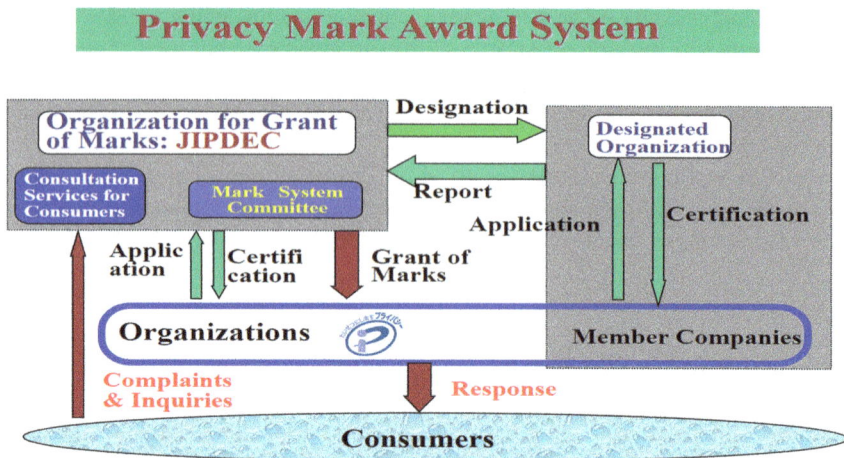

Fig. 5.5 Privacy Mark Program 2001 [Source: Yamadori, Yuji. JIPDEC. Privacy Mark Award System, March 2001 presentation. https://www.pcpd.org.hk/misc/japan/Japan.ppt. Accessed 17 December 2017]

March 2015, JIPDEC reports that almost 19,000 organisations have been granted a PrivacyMark.[37]

Since its inception, the PrivacyMark program has evolved over the last 15+ years. Figure 5.5 reflects the organisation and process in 2001.

The PrivacyMark program has grown to a full governance structure. The program is administered by JIPDEC as the granting organisation to grant the use of PrivacyMark and various assessment bodies. There are a set of guidelines and requirements to be approved as an Assessment Body. A committee made up of scholars, specialists, representatives from business associations, consumers and legal professionals oversees the establishment and revision of standards and regulations to operate PrivacyMark System, designation and revocation of an assessment body and revocation of the use of the PrivacyMark. JIPDEC provides responses to consumer inquiries and complaints of PrivacyMark entities. Users are also able to click on the PrivacyMark logo on a website to determine the validity of the organisation's use of the PrivacyMark.[38]

The logo or seal (see Fig. 5.6) itself also includes a set of rules for use. Included in the logo is a 10-digit registration number assigned by JIPDEC and/or any one of the approved Assessment Bodies. AA (This two-digit number signifies the code of the Assessment Body, e.g., JIPDEC ("10")). The next 6 digits is a persistent unique organisation ID. This last two-digit number beginning "01" signifies the number of two-year renewals.

---

[37] JIPDEC 2016.

[38] Yamadori 2001.

Fig. 5.6 PrivacyMark Logo
[Source: JIPDEC, https://
privacymark.org. Accessed 17
December 2017]

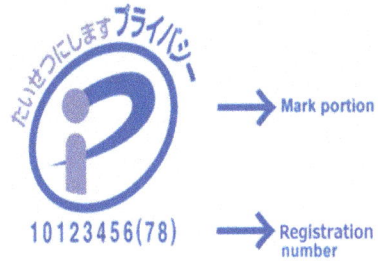

A PrivacyMark assessment involves both document review and an on-site assessment. The document review stage assesses over 120 items in an organization's personal information protection management system. The onsite assessment reviews over 52 items of the organisation's operations and over 41 security safeguards. The PrivacyMark program includes three designated organisations approved to operate training for assessors. As of March 2015, there are 1,209 assessors registered (senior assessor, assessor, assistant assessor).

Figure 5.7 reflects the organisation and process for the PrivacyMark in 2016.

There are also privacy breach reporting requirements, of which, any breaches involving highly sensitive personal information must be reported directly to the Minister. There is a system to rate the penalty for a breach and the penalty level is based on several points based on, for example, organisation due diligence/

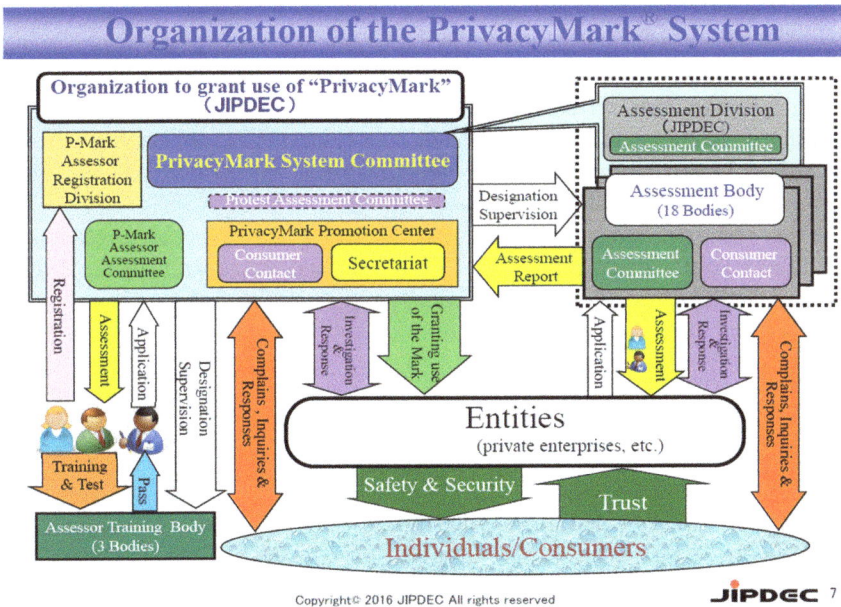

Fig. 5.7 Organisation and Process for the PrivacyMark in 2017 [Source: JIPDEC. The PrivacyMark System. 2017. https://privacymark.org/ou0ioa000000013f-att/ThePrivacyMarkSystem.pdf. Accessed 17 December 2017]

responsibility; type and volume of personal information involved in the breach; the history of breaches within the organisation.

Fees are based on the size of the organisation (small, medium, large) and whether it is a new application or a renewal. The fee includes an amount for processing the application (whether new or renewal), for undertaking the screening/assessment and lastly, for the use of the PrivacyMark logo. As of 1 April 2014, the fee for a new application ranges from 308,573 JpnYen to 1,234,286 JpnYen. For a renewal, the fees range from 226,286 JpnYen to 925,715 JpnYen.[39] The fee is for a two-year period.

5.6 Canada

In January 2000, the Canadian E-Business Opportunities Roundtable identified six areas in which Canada should strive to establish e-business leadership. The sixth area was to build a global reputation regarding Internet policy development "by establishing a Canadian-branded, internationally recognized consumer protection mark and forum for dispute resolution".[40]

The Roundtable suggested that the development of the consumer protection mark, or trust mark, be led by the private sector through consultation with interested parties such as the retail business sector, consumer groups, government, and the Canadian Standards Association (CSA) International. CSA is the standards body whose Model Code for the Protection of Personal Information is the core of Canadian federal privacy legislation. Once established in Canada, the view was that the trust mark would be transformed quickly "into an international standard providing a higher-level accreditation recognized across borders". The Roundtable envisioned the trust mark being managed by a neutral third party tasked to build awareness, promote adoption of the program, track compliance, and provide a system for dispute resolution.

What follows is an update on Chartered Professional Accountants (CPA) WebTrust and an overview of a newly launched seal program by the Privacy and Big Data Institute at Ryerson University.

5.6.1 CPA WebTrust

This seal was developed jointly by the American Institute of Certified Public Accountants (AICPA) and the Canadian Institute of Chartered Accountants (CICA), now the Chartered Professional Accountants (CPA) Canada. CPA

---

[39] http://privacymark.org/application/cost/index.html. Accessed 1 June 2016.

[40] The Boston Consulting Group (Canada) 2000.

WebTrust was launched in September 1997 by the American Institute of Certified Public Accountants (AICPA). Since its launch, there is evidence that WebTrust evolved and enhanced its criteria for privacy and consumer protection to meet guidelines established by the Online Privacy Alliance (OPA) in the United States. To further build consumer confidence with the program, a consumer arbitration program was added.

In its research, the authors were advised by CPA Canada that the CPA WebTrust Privacy Seal program was discontinued several years ago. According to frequently asked questions (FAQs) on AICPA's website, the WebTrust Consumer Protection Seal was available in the past for entities that met the Trust Services Processing Integrity and Online Privacy Principles, however, this special seal and related practitioner's report was seldom used and is now discontinued. The website FAQs note, however, a WebTrust seal, without the "Consumer Protection" designation could still be issued. When the privacy engagement relates to an online segment, an entity may choose to display a WebTrust Online Privacy seal. For these engagements, the scope needs to include, as a minimum, an online business segment of the entity.[41]

5.6.2 Privacy by Design Certification Shield

Launched in May 2015, Privacy by Design Certification[42] was established by the Privacy and Big Data Institute at Ryerson University, Toronto, Canada. The basis for Ryerson's Privacy by Design Certification are the seven Foundational Principles of Privacy by Design. Created by Dr. Ann Cavoukian, Privacy by Design is a framework that seeks to proactively embed privacy into the design specifications of information technologies, networked infrastructure and business practices, thereby achieving the strongest protection possible. The certification program is overseen by an advisory board.

The Institute partnered with Deloitte who was responsible for translating the seven Foundational Principles into 29 measurable privacy criteria and 109 illustrative privacy controls using a unique scorecard approach that aligns to Privacy by Design. The criteria and controls are based on key requirements derived from national and international privacy regulations and best practices.

As a first step, organisations will apply online to Ryerson's Privacy and Big Data Institute. Then, using a set of well-defined assessment criteria, Deloitte's privacy and security professionals test an organisation's product, service or offering against the seven Foundational Principles of Privacy by Design. An assessment of the strength of an organisation's privacy practices is conducted, following

---

[41] Refer to FAQs on the AICPA website—http://www.aicpa.org. Accessed 1 June 2016.

[42] Refer to the Privacy by Design Certification website. https://www.ryerson.ca/pbdce/certification/. Accessed 17 December 2017.

Fig. 5.8 Privacy by Design
Certification Shield [Source:
Cavoukian A, Commit to
Privacy, Publicly: Privacy by
Design Certification Program.
https://www.ryerson.ca/
content/dam/pbdce/
certification/PbD-
Brochure.pdf. Accessed
17 December 2017]

internationally-recognised privacy principles, including privacy regulations, industry self-regulatory requirements and industry best practices (e.g., FIPs, OECD, GAPP, CBR and APEC Privacy Framework) using an assessment methodology based on harmonized privacy and security requirements. The approach is described as holistic and risk-based.

Upon successful completion, Deloitte issues an assessment report to the organisation. Only when Ryerson is satisfied that no significant gaps exist as identified by Deloitte in the Privacy Scorecard, the organisation is granted permission to display the Privacy by Design Certification Shield, see Fig. 5.8. A Certification Shield use agreement must be signed by the organisation and sets out the terms and conditions for use of the Shield.

PbD Certification is valid for three years from the initial date of certification, however, certification is subject to a yearly renewal. To maintain certification, the organisation must pay the renewal fee plus taxes on the first and second anniversary of certification, and complete the attestation form.

5.7 India—'DSCI Privacy Certified' (DPC©)

Established in 1988, NASSCOM is India's National Association of Software and Service Companies and responsible for establishing the Data Security Council of India (DSCI). As noted in several of its reports, DSCI is an independent, not-for-profit organisation with a focus on building a credible and committed self-regulatory organisation to uphold data privacy and security standards. DSCI's mission is to build trust in Indian companies as global sourcing service providers, and to send out a message to clients worldwide that India is a secure destination for outsourcing, where privacy and protection of customer data are enshrined in the global best practices followed by the industry.

According to DSCI, it builds capacity in security, privacy and cyber forensics through training and certification program for professionals and law enforcement agencies and engages stakeholders through various outreach initiatives including events, awards, chapters, consultations and membership programs. See Fig. 5.9 for an illustration of the DSCI certification process.

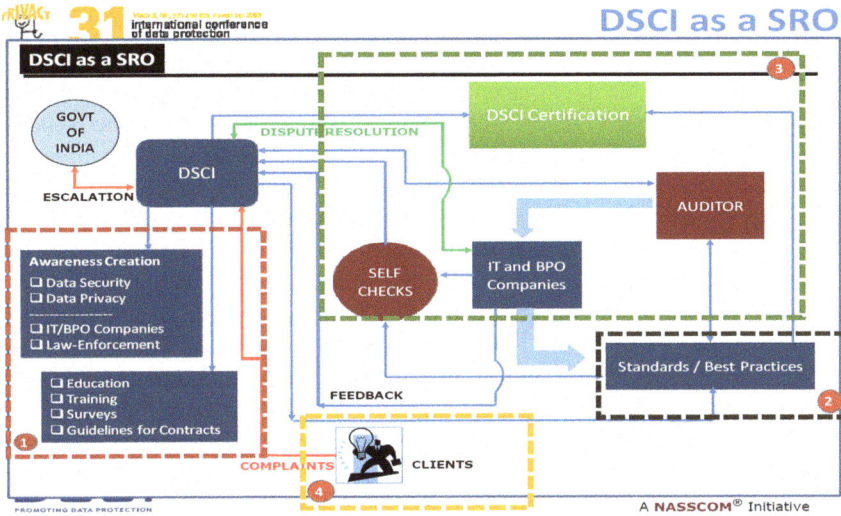

Fig. 5.9 Illustration of the DSCI certification process within its self-regulatory framework Source: Bajaj, K. Standards for Privacy Protection: DSCI approach. Presentation to 31st Intal Conference of Privacy Commissioners, November 2009]

DSCI best practices for data protection are reflected in two frameworks: the DSCI Data Security Framework comprises 16 Best Practices and is based on the ISO 27001 security standard, and other standards such as PCI DSS; the DSCI Privacy Framework is based on nine Best Practices and 12 Privacy Principles that DSCI notes: "satisfy the requirements of Privacy laws and data protection directives of the European Union, the United States, and APEC countries."[43]

DSCI released its Security Framework (DSF©) and Privacy Framework (DPF©) in 2010. DSCI saw the need for assessment frameworks, that would help organizations conduct their own analysis and launched the DSCI Assessment Framework-Security (DAF-S©) and DSCI Assessment Framework-Privacy (DAF-P©) in 2012. DSCI notes that at the moment, undertaking these self-assessments will not qualify for certification. According to a 2014 DSCI press release and listed on Vodafone India's website, Vodafone India Limited (VIL)—Delhi Circle, became one of the first telecom companies in India to be certified as a 'DSCI Privacy Certified' (DPC©) organisation.

DSCI uses an authorised Assessment Organization (AO) to conduct the requirements of DSCI Privacy Framework (DPF©) and DSCI Assessment Framework for Privacy (DAF-P©). It is not clear what the certification fees are except that a DSCI membership brochure does note that membership privileges include "Consultation & Advisory: Consultation on security & privacy queries and for implementation of DSCI Frameworks."

---

[43] https://www.dsci.in/taxonomypage/297. Accessed 1 May 2017.

5.8 Australia

Despite looking into the development of a privacy web seal, to date, there has been little formal Government action with regard to web seals. In 1999, the National Office for the Information Economy (NOIE) and the Commonwealth Department of the Treasury convened a round table discussion.[44] The Roundtable resulted in identifying some of the issues that needed to be addressed—for example, it was noted that to be effective, a seal should have international recognition, be comprehensive and affordable, be backed by an audit process and an effective redress mechanism. However, further work in this area appears to have lapsed. A year later, an Australian senate committee[45] recommended the development of a privacy web seal by the federal privacy commissioner to certify that a site offers "the highest level of privacy protection from the consumers' point of view." It would use Australia's National Privacy Principles as a minimum, but would be more stringent in some respect.[46]

According to a report prepared by the Australian Commerce Department, in 2000, the Federal Government adopted the E-commerce Best Practice Model Building Consumer Sovereignty in Electronic Commerce: A Best Practice Model for Business.[47] The Best Practice Model translates the OECD Guidelines for the Australian context. It does not purport to be a web seal scheme but aims to set best practice standards for online consumer protection. This report did identify an Australian web seal program known as "eTick" with a mission "to be the global new economy certification authority establishing benchmarks for eCommerce standards internationally".[48] Established in 2001, the report noted that it suffered a financial collapse in 2002 and was eventually withdrawn.[49]

In the latter part of 2015, the independent and international Biometrics Institute in Australia received funding from the Australian government to take its Biometrics Privacy Trust Mark development to the next stage.[50] The Biometrics Institute had announced in the latter part of 2014 that it was consulting with its members and key stakeholders about the development of a Biometrics Institute Trust Mark. The Biometrics Institute was established in October 2001 with a mission is to promote the responsible use of biometrics. The Institute's website notes that "privacy principles in some form will be integral to the successful implementation of biometric technology, particularly in terms of the use and disclosure of the public's

---

[44] Connolly 2008.

[45] Australian Senate Select Committee on Information Technologies 2000.

[46] MacDonnell 2001.

[47] Australian Dept of Justice 2002.

[48] Australian Dept of Justice 2002.

[49] Connolly 2008.

[50] Trust Mark Australian Biometrics Institute http://www.biometricsinstitute.org/pages/trust-mark.html. Accessed 1 June 2016.

personal information." As of March 2016, information sourced from their website notes that the Biometrics Institute is working on the details of the Trust Mark through member and stakeholder consultations.

5.9   Conclusion

A privacy seal or icon is an extension of or one tool in the arsenal of measures (e.g., legal instruments, technical standards, public education, expert consultation and moral suasion)[51] to protect the privacy of consumers in the online world. Nonetheless, such a visual identifier continues to be of interest and its significance is reflected in Europe's inclusion of such a mechanism in its General Data Protection Regulation and efforts by APEC to provide regulatory oversight of privacy seal providers by making them eligible to be an "accountability agent". The results of the scan of the six jurisdictions and their respective privacy seal initiatives help us to understand the complexity and depth of the process behind what appears to be a simple mark or icon. In the 2000 report initiated by the international data protection authorities and at a time when privacy seals were at a nascent stage, the future role that seals might play in e-commerce was unclear. The conclusion of the report was that privacy seals could come into their own as a powerful facilitator of globalisation of consumer transactions if they are able to provide acceptable and enforceable privacy protection across multiple jurisdictions. Despite the years that have passed, the authors see that progress has been made and that work such as this and the other chapters in this book contributes the necessary assessment to achieve this goal.

References

APEC (2009) APEC Data Privacy Pathfinder Projects Implementation Work Plan – Revised. First Technical Assistance Seminar on the Implementation of the APEC Data Privacy Pathfinder, Singapore 22–23 February 2009

Article 29 Data Protection Working Party (2010) Opinion 3/2010 on the principle of accountability. http://ec.europa.eu/justice/policies/privacy/docs/wpdocs/2010/wp173_en.pdf. Accessed 1 June 2016

Australian Department of Justice (2002) Web Seals of Approval Discussion Paper. Business and Consumer Affairs Victoria. https://www.consumer.vic.gov.au/.../web-seals-of-approval-2002.pdf. Accessed 1 June 2016

Australian Senate Select Committee on Information Technologies (2000) "Cookie Monsters? Privacy in the information society." http://www.aph.gov.au/binaries/senate/committee/it_ctte/completed_inquiries/1999-02/e_privacy/report/report.pdf. Accessed 1 June 2016

---

[51] Cavoukian and Crompton 2000.

Baja K (undated) Data Security Council of India (DSCI): A self-regulatory organization. Paper for Industry Consultation. https://www.dsci.in/sites/default/files/DSCI%20Privacy%20SRO.pdf. Accessed 1 June 2016

Bennett CJ (2004) Privacy Self-Regulation in a Global Economy: A Race to the Top, the Bottom or Somewhere Else? In: Kernaghan W (ed) Voluntary Codes: Private Governance, the Public Interest and Innovation. Carleton Research Unit for Innovation, Science and Environment, Carleton University, pp 227–248

The Boston Consulting Group (Canada) (2000) Fast Forward: Accelerating Canada's Leadership in the Internet Economy. http://www.crc.gc.ca/reports/roundtable_e.pdf. Accessed 1 June 2016

Cavoukian A, Crompton M (2000) Web Seals: A review of online privacy programs. A Joint Project of the Office of the Information and Privacy Commissioner/Ontario and the Office of the Federal Privacy Commissioner of Australia. 22nd International Conference on Privacy and Personal Data Protection

Connolly C (2008) Trustmark Schemes Struggle to Protect Privacy. Galexia Pty Ltd. Australia. http://www.galexia.com/public/research/assets/trustmarks_struggle_20080926/. Accessed 1 June 2016

Federal Trade Commission (1999) Self-regulation and Privacy Online: A Report to Congress. https://www.ftc.gov/reports/self-regulation-privacy-onlinea-federal-trade-commission-report-congress. Accessed 1 June 2016

JIPDEC (2016) The PrivacyMark System: System, Reliability mechanism, Transparency and Mutual programs. A presentation by the PrivacyMark Promotion Center. http://privacymark.org/. Accessed 1 June 2016

MacDonnell J (2001) Exporting Trust: Does e-commerce need a Canadian privacy seal of approval? The Alberta Law Review 39:346–437

Newman P (undated) A brief history of ethical stamps and seals. FairTruth Certified Elfenworks. http://elfenworks.org/a-brief-history-of-ethical-stamps-and-seals/. Accessed 1 June 2016

Rifon N, LaRose R, Choi SM (2005) Your Privacy is Sealed: Effects of Web Privacy Seals on Trust and Personal Disclosures. Journal of Consumer Affairs 39:339–362

Rodrigues R, Barnard-Wils D, Wright D, De Hert P, Papakonstantinou V (2013) EU Privacy Seals Project: Inventory and analysis of privacy certification schemes. In: Beslay L, Dubois N (eds) European Commission Final Report Study Deliverable 1.4

Yamadori Y (2001) Privacy Mark Award System. Japan Information Processing Development Corporation. https://www.pcpd.org.hk/misc/japan/Japan.ppt. Accessed 1 June 2016

Chapter 6
Controversies and Challenges of Trustmarks: Lessons for Privacy and Data Protection Seals

Paolo Balboni and Theodora Dragan

Contents

Prof. Dr. Paolo Balboni, Founding Partner of ICT Legal Consulting; Professor of Privacy, Cybersecurity, and IT Contract Law at the European Centre on Privacy and Cybersecurity within the Maastricht University Faculty of Law; and President of the European Privacy Association. Theodora Dragan, Fellow of the European Privacy Association.

P. Balboni (✉)
European Centre on Privacy and Cybersecurity, Maastricht University Faculty of Law, Maastricht, The Netherlands
e-mail: paolo.balboni@maastrichtuniversity.nl

P. Balboni
ICT Legal Consulting, Milan, Italy

P. Balboni · T. Dragan
European Privacy Association, Brussels, Belgium

© T.M.C. ASSER PRESS and the authors 2018
R. Rodrigues and V. Papakonstantinou (eds.), *Privacy and Data Protection Seals*, Information Technology and Law Series 28, https://doi.org/10.1007/978-94-6265-228-6_6

Abstract While trustmarks have already existed for many years, until now very few have managed to successfully establish themselves on the market in terms of consumer trust and adoption by online businesses. This chapter will deal with the challenges and controversies related to trustmarks and will highlight some significant lessons learned from the experience with trustmarks. Based on this, it will identify key factors that can contribute to the success of privacy and data protection seals in the years to come. The chapter will combine theoretical knowledge with empirical observations to establish a reliable yardstick to measure the effectiveness and impact of trustmarks and, finally, will identify the legal challenges that need to be overcome for trustmarks to gain and maintain relevance in the fast-paced world of e-commerce.

Keywords Data protection seals · trustmarks · kitemark · online trust · privacy · e-commerce

6.1   The Role of Trustmarks in e-Commerce

> The Committee believes that one way to increase consumer trust in online platforms is the creation of a traffic-light style kite-mark on all websites and apps, to show good practice on privacy policies. This, we believe, will encourage platforms to compete against each other to improve standards on transparency, privacy and use of personal data (Lord Whitty, Chairman of The House of Lords EU Committee European Union Committee commenting on the report on Online Platforms and the Digital Single Market, 20 April 2016).[1]

The first trustmarks were introduced in the 1990s with the aim of bridging the gap between the e-seller and the e-buyer and to contribute to the development of cross-border e-commerce. E-commerce has significantly grown over time. In 2014, 180 billion euros were spent by 247 million European consumers in online shopping according to a study conducted by PostNord, but despite such sustained

---

[1] The House of Lords 2016.

growth, it remains an insufficiently explored field.[2] This is due to a number of reasons, of which the five most frequently mentioned are: security, privacy, unfamiliarity with services, lack of direct interaction, and credibility of information.[3] Trustmarks were therefore developed in response to some of these concerns to give consumers confidence when purchasing and sellers more exposure and incentives to place products on the online market, thus stimulating the creation of a wider, better, and stronger e-commerce market.

Nevertheless, a study by the European Union found that in 2014 a mere 19% of enterprises made electronic sales, therefore concluding that "cross border e-commerce sales [are] not fully exploited by enterprises selling electronically".[4] Despite the fact that e-commerce enables companies to access markets outside the country of origin, and provides the potential to reshape the European Single Market by allowing price and product-related comparisons beyond country borders, e-consumers still do not trust the e-commerce environment.

What are the reasons for this lack of trust and how exactly can trustmarks help in this respect?

Distrust of the e-commerce market stems from the very different risk allocation in both traditional and online shopping. Traditionally, a shopping experience involves a buyer who visits the shop of a seller and compares the various objects for sale, touching and weighing them against each other before deciding to pay for an item and immediately obtaining it. The buyer incurs almost no risk; instead, the seller must be careful about the quality of the products offered for sale and the customer service if he wants to increase his chances of making a sale. The Internet took this model and turned it on its head, completely overhauling the shopping experience. The buyer can still look at the various items online, but in the case of e-commerce, he or she is conditioned to make a decision based on pictures posted by the owner of the e-shop, not on his or her own perception of the items. Furthermore, the buyer has to pay the purchase price and rely on the fact that the unknown seller will deliver the product by the specified time, that the purchased item will arrive intact, and that the payment details will not be intercepted by malicious third parties. It is rather easy to see that the e-shopping experience, although similar to the traditional one, involves greater risks for the buyer, who finds him or herself in a more vulnerable position.

In the attempt to address this vulnerability, trustmarks create a connection between the buyer and the (trustmark-approved) seller. Scott David, a Washington University identity management legal expert, explains the phenomenon with reference to supply chains, in which trust is similarly important for determining a participant to take a risk: "In supply chains there is a sufficient natural affinity among stakeholders for supply chain integrity and risk reduction through participant discipline. Supply chain discipline is enhanced through the use of certification

---

[2] PostNord 2015, p. 5.

[3] European Consumer Centres Network 2013, p. 7.

[4] Eurostat 2015.

marks that enable instant recognition of conformity to mutually-agreed-upon supply chain participant requirements."[5] In this sense trustmarks are community tools that offer advantages to e-sellers and e-buyers alike, creating the connection that would be easy to find in traditional commerce, but that is not as easy to establish in the context of e-commerce.

In an ideal world, the introduction of trustmarks would directly correlate with an increase of the public's trust in e-commerce and, thus, with a stronger e-commerce market. However, the Organisation for Economic Co-operation and Development (OECD) found that, despite the proliferation of trustmark schemes, trust in e-commerce is still affected by several problems that both businesses and consumers experience.[6] These problems have been divided into two categories, consisting of practical and regulatory barriers. Practical barriers include "language problems, time required for businesses to set up an effective e-commerce platform, and a lack of interoperability of delivery and payment systems," whilst regulatory barriers include "complex VAT systems, overlapping frameworks addressing e-commerce issues (including consumer, privacy, intellectual property, telecommunication and competition rules), or regulatory gaps."[7] Many of these issues have been addressed by trustmark schemes aimed precisely at solving these problems. For example, the display of a trustmark as a visual symbol is aimed at breaking the language barrier and fostering intra-EU trade—the *EMOTA* trustmark[8] does just that, by placing its "umbrella" seal next to the seal of a specific country. Another example is that some trustmark schemes were developed specifically to help e-traders to comply with specific regulations and show their compliance by displaying a privacy seal. For example, *EuroPriSe*[9] developed a step-by-step privacy compliance plan that must be followed before the seal is awarded.

So why is e-commerce still lagging behind, if trustmarks and seals and badges were introduced to address the specific problems that were identified by researchers?

Until now, the role of trustmarks in e-commerce has been an uncertain one, characterised by high ambitions (solving most of the problems of e-commerce at once) and low impact (a survey by the European Consumer Centres Network in 2013 found that 51% of 573 respondents do not know what a trustmark is and 66% do not know any trustmark).[10] This is mainly because trustmarks first have to become established on the market to command trust and very few have managed to do so, whilst the rest are finding themselves in ambiguous, ambivalent territory.

---

[5] Rosner 2014, p. 8.

[6] OECD Digital Economy Papers 2013, p. 17.

[7] OECD Digital Economy Papers 2013, p. 17.

[8] EMOTA Trustmark, more information available at: http://www.emota.eu/#!ecommercetrustmark/c1jas. Accessed 26 April 2016.

[9] EuroPriSe Trustmark, more information available at: https://www.european-privacy-seal.eu/EPS-en/Certification. Accessed 26 April 2016.

[10] European Consumer Centres Network 2013, pp. 15–16, figures 1.1 and 1.2.

For this reason, consumers do not easily recognise them on websites and businesses do not actively use them, which makes it difficult for trustmarks to make an impact and gain prominence. A project conducted by the European Consumer Center Network (ECC-Net) found that "surprisingly few traders use trustmarks"—out of the 340 websites used, only 17% displayed a trustmark.[11] To be effective, trustmark schemes need to reach a critical mass.[12] To reach a critical mass, they need to be deployed on many websites at the same time. It may look like a vicious circle, but this chapter sets out to break it by identifying the controversial aspects of trustmarks and pinpointing potential approaches that could lead to the trustmarks gaining the reputation needed to become relevant elements of the e-commerce market.

This said, trustmarks seem to have another great chance to play a fundamental role in the development of European e-commerce and enhancement of personal data protection: "[t]he Committee believes that one way to increase consumer trust in online platforms is the creation of a traffic-light style kite-mark on all websites and apps, to show good practice on privacy policies. This, we believe, will encourage platforms to compete against each other to improve standards on transparency, privacy and use of personal data." (Lord Whitty, Chairman of The House of Lords EU Committee European Union Committee commenting on the report on Online Platforms and the Digital Single Market, 20 April 2016.)[13]

6.2 Structure and Methodology

This chapter explores the challenges of trustmarks from a privacy and business law perspective, combining theoretical observations on the meaning of trust, the functions of trustmarks and the value attributed to them, with empirical research on the trustmark schemes in the European Union (EU). The chapter starts with a section that contains the theoretical analysis of the function of trustmarks, focusing on the dichotomy between their intended function and their perceived function. The second part of the chapter looks at the business and legal aspects of the major trustmark providers in the EU, organised in macro categories according to their governance schemes. It identifies the main controversies for each specific cluster and suggests potential solutions coherent with the respective business practices, taking into account the needs of all stakeholders. Finally, the chapter closes with an objective evaluation of the European trustmark landscape and provides an integrated analysis of how the controversies may be solved and the challenges may be overcome.

---

[11] European Consumer Centres Network 2011, p. 20.

[12] Rule 2002, p. 107.

[13] The House of Lords 2016.

6.3 The Characteristics of Trustmarks

The average consumer does not have the time and resources to perform thorough checks on each e-merchant that offers the goods or services that they may be looking for. Trustmarks propose to do this on their behalf, relieving them of a burden and at the same time providing the e-merchants with a way of convincing potential e-consumers to purchase from their online stores or sign up for their services without worrying. Trustmarks play an important role in the online world, as they can visually convey the conformity of an e-merchant with specific security, privacy or business practices. As the name implies, trustmarks are meant to convey the idea that the e-merchant is *to be trusted* because he or she complies with practices such as those mentioned above. The visual characteristic of the trustmark enables the consumers to quickly associate a trader with a pre-determined set of characteristics that they would not have any proof of otherwise. In this way the trader essentially bypasses the step of convincing each potential individual consumer of its trustworthiness, by implying it instead through its affiliation with a certification scheme.[14] According to a paper on trust by psychology scholars Mayer, Davis and Schoorman, "*CTIS* [ed.: consumer trust in internet shopping] is defined as the willingness of a consumer to be vulnerable to the actions of an Internet merchant in an Internet shopping transaction, based on the expectation that the Internet merchant will behave in certain agreeable ways, irrespective of the ability of the consumer to monitor or control the Internet merchant".[15] In case of a webpage displaying a trustmark, the e-consumers' expectation that the e-merchant will behave in a specific way is indicated by the fact that the e-merchant has been found to be likely to behave in such way by the trustmark provider, based on a list of criteria that can usually be consulted on the trustmark provider's website. As such, trustmarks have the capacity of making the unknown seem familiar, thus stimulating consumers to make a purchase in circumstances in which they otherwise may not.

---

[14] "Data Protection. The report concludes that consumer trust in online platforms is 'worryingly low' because consumers do not fully understand how online platforms collect and use personal data, and that there is a lack of competition between platforms on privacy standards. The Committee recommends that a kite-mark is created for websites and applications to indicate to consumers the quality of their privacy policies. In order to foster competition and drive up privacy standards, this kite-mark should include a graded, traffic light style, scale. Harnessing the power of corporate reputation, the report recommends that online platforms should be required to notify users when they are found to have breached privacy rules." The House of Lords EU Committee European Union Committee's report on Online Platforms and the Digital Single Market, 20 April 2016. Available at: http://www.publications.parliament.uk/pa/ld201516/ldselect/ldeucom/129/12902.htm. Accessed 26 April 2016.

[15] Mayer et al. 1995, pp. 709–734.

6.3.1   Main Function: Triggering Trust by Making the Unknown Appear Familiar

The main function of trustmarks is to encourage e-consumers to use the services of a particular e-merchant based on the fact that the e-merchant has been found to be trustworthy by the trustmark provider according to a list of criteria that can usually be consulted on the trustmark provider's website. In this way, e-consumers perceive that the risk of an online transaction is moved from themselves to the organisation that certified the e-merchant; this may be the reason why consumers who see a trustmark displayed on a website more likely to make a purchase, according to a survey conducted by Econsultancy/Toluna.[16] Shankar et al.[17] describe online trust as "a reliance on a firm by its stakeholders with regard to its business activities in the electronic medium, and in particular, its website". Such reliance, as explained above, can be achieved in two ways: either e-consumers autonomously decide to trust the website and proceed with a transaction, or the e-consumers trust a third party (the trustmark provider) and, by association, the e-merchant that was certified by the third party. In the first case, the e-consumers' decision to make a purchase is entirely their own, based on their own reasoning and considerations; any risks have been weighted independently by themselves and, should something go wrong, the responsibility is entirely theirs. In the second case, the e-consumers' decision is, to some extent, based on their reliance on the trustmark provider. There is thus a shift of the e-consumers' trust from the e-merchant to the trustmark provider, and so the function of trustmarks is to activate that shift.

In the first scenario, where the e-consumers rely on their own decision of trusting the website to make a purchase, they bear the risk of that transaction and of the related problems. In the second scenario, the e-consumers decide to trust the website because the trustmark persuades them to do so; should they still bear the entire risk of the purchase? It would seem that the risk should, at the very least, be divided equally between e-consumer, e-merchant and trustmark provider; however, trustmark providers expressly exclude liability in the terms and conditions published on their respective websites. The perceptive reader will have already identified the first controversial issue: **trustmark providers should not be able to certify that a website corresponds to certain standards but then fully exclude liability in case of non-conformities**.[18]

A mystery shopping project carried out by ECC-Net found that out of the fifty-two websites that were part of the project and displayed a trustmark, only forty-four traders gave the consumer a refund and only twenty-one refunded the delivery costs for shipping the item from the trader to the consumer.[19] The other

---

[16] E-Consultancy 2011.

[17] Shankar et al. 2002, pp. 325–344.

[18] See Balboni 2009, pp. 207ss.

[19] European Consumer Centres Network 2011, p. 20.

twenty-three traders that displayed a trustmark did not provide a refund in accordance with Article 6(1) of the Distance Selling Directive[20] (now replaced by the Directive on Consumer Rights 2011/83/EC).[21] Although it may be argued that those twenty-three wrongly displayed trustmarks were certifying the respective websites for criteria other than compliance with e-commerce regulations, it is nevertheless obvious that those trustmarks were not clear enough about it, leading the average consumer to believe that they certified the trustworthiness of the website in general, and that some action would be taken if the trustworthiness were to be proven wrong.

Let us focus for a moment on the triangle of stakeholders involved: the e-consumer, the e-merchant and the trustmark provider. If things go well, the e-consumer successfully completes a transaction on the e-merchant's website, which is certified by the trustmark provider. The trustmark provider can use this as an example of a successful transaction supported by the trustmark, therefore using it as a selling point for its own brand and making a gain out of it. However, what if in the course of the transaction a cyber threat is activated and the e-consumer's data is stolen? What if the certified website undertakes to comply with a certification scheme, but then fails to set up the infrastructure to do so in practice? No evidence whatsoever (in the form of statements, press releases etc.) has been found to show that a trustmark provider has taken any responsibility for an error connected with the trustmark. Looking at the studies presented above and taking into consideration that trustmarks have existed for about twenty years, it seems unlikely that trustmarks were *never* the reason why a customer decided to go through with a transaction that proved to be bad in hindsight.

6.3.2 Controversies Related to the "Trust Trigger" Function of the Trustmarks

Having established that trustmarks have the capacity to make the unknown seem familiar by activating a shift in the perception of the average consumer that determines him or her to project onto a website the characteristics represented by the trustmark, but that the trustmark providers exclude all liability in case of bad purchases, it seems that there are some controversial questions that need to be answered.

---

[20] Directive 97/7/EC of the European Parliament and of the Council of 20 May 1997 on the protection of consumers in respect of distance contracts.

[21] Directive 2011/83/EU of the European Parliament and of the Council of 25 October 2011 on consumer rights, amending Council Directive 93/13/EEC and Directive 1999/44/EC of the European Parliament and of the Council and repealing Council Directive 85/577/EEC and Directive 97/7/EC of the European Parliament and of the Council.

- Who is to be held responsible in situations when things go wrong?
- Is the trustmark provider liable for not having conducted enough checks?
- Is responsibility shared between the e-consumer, the e-merchant and the trustmark provider?
- Is the consumer to bear responsibility for having relied upon the trustmark that was displayed?
- Should there be a general approach to this issue or should each single instance be dealt with on a case-by-case basis?

The allocation of the risk in an e-commerce transaction is a recurring *leitmotiv*[22] that will be analysed from different perspectives throughout the chapter. In the first place, however, the answer is very closely connected to the inherent function of the trustmark and understanding the underlying principles will enable the reader to proceed with these considerations in a systematic manner.

If the function of a trustmark is to proactively encourage the e-consumer to make a purchase and therefore to increase sales for an e-merchant, then such a trustmark is a merchant-centric tool. It enables the merchant to generate more sales and increase the profit margin and is therefore likely to be acquired by the e-merchant, who has an interest in growing his business and can see the tangible return on investment provided by the trustmark scheme. Both the e-merchant and the trustmark provider are at an advantage, because they both stand to make a profit—the merchant through online sales and the trustmark provider through the subscription costs that are paid by the merchant. Consumers, however, are at a disadvantage due to the financial incentive of the trustmark provider, who may be tempted to overlook a small non-compliance of an e-merchant to retain their client, or may hesitate before adding them to a blacklist for the same reason.[23]

If instead the function of a trustmark is to show, with as much transparency and accuracy as possible, that an e-merchant is carefully following the privacy, security, business principles or industry standards, then such a trustmark is a consumer-centric tool. It helps the e-consumer decide which online businesses to trust and to rely on and places a "burden" on online businesses to comply with specific standards, sanctioning them if they do not fully comply. In this scenario, the e-consumers are at an advantage, because they feel comfortable carrying out online transactions, in the knowledge that the trustmark provider has thoroughly checked every single aspect of the website and that such verifications are always up to date. If trustmark compliance is made very difficult by trustmark providers, then online traders will not have an incentive to collaborate with such providers and will not subscribe to their schemes. In the long run, there will be fewer trustmark-certified websites and this will reflect on the consumers, who will have to use their own time and resources to establish the trustworthiness of a website.

---

[22] *Leitmotiv* is a recurrent theme that is associated with a particular person or idea.

[23] For example, the reliability of the US trustmark provider TRUSTe was widely criticised because "despite having handled thousands of disputes, to date [it] has never revoked a single seal", Cortés 2011, p. 63.

It is quite clear that the two scenarios presented above do not fully satisfy the needs of the e-consumers, e-merchants and trustmark providers. The merchant-centric model puts the consumer in a vulnerable position, whilst the consumer-centric model removes the incentives of traders to sign up for a trustmark scheme. What is needed is a third model, a neutral approach that would reconcile the interests of the e-merchants and e-consumers, at the same enabling the trustmark provider to develop a sustainable business model. If trustmarks are to establish and maintain a reputation in the long run, trustmark providers will need to focus on delivering a reliable service, even if that may include performing strict checks from time to time or sanctioning businesses that do not comply with the code of conduct.

6.4 Trustmarks and Data Protection Seals in the European Union

6.4.1 Challenges

As of 2016, there were approximately thirty active trustmark schemes within the EU as shown by the empirical research we carried out while writing this chapter. The number is likely to vary from time to time and, potentially, to increase in the near-future due to the enactment of the Regulation (EU) 2016/679,[24] which encourages the creation of certification schemes. The empirical research that was conducted shows that the majority of trustmark schemes active at the moment were founded between 2001 and 2006 and that the trustmark landscape is highly fragmented. According to the European Consumer Centres Network's common "Can I trust the trust mark?" report, which was made public in Brussels on 16 October 2013, navigating the European trustmark landscape is comparable to "confronting an impenetrable jungle".[25]

Trustmark schemes are in a difficult position in the European Union. No single trustmark or privacy seal has reached critical mass so far; ironically, however, the proliferation of trustmarks has brought confusion and a lack of harmonisation—making it even harder for a trustmark to establish itself. Unless consumers are educated about the meaning and value of trustmarks and about the process of awarding a seal, the trustmark as a tool will not be taken seriously. Organising educational campaigns and offering access to free, easy to understand information would be a first step in this direction.

---

[24] REGULATION (EU) 2016/679 OF THE EUROPEAN PARLIAMENT AND OF THE COUNCIL of the 27th of April 2016 on the protection of natural persons with regard to the processing of personal data and on the free movement of such data, and repealing Directive 95/46/EC (General Data Protection Regulation).

[25] European Consumer Center Network 2013, p. 57.

One reason for the difficult position of the trustmarks was already identified in a research conducted in 2005; the researchers found that most of the trustmark schemes available at the time were characterised by a "lack of European sensitivity".[26] By this expression, the researchers referred to the lack of multilingual information, the lack of coordination between the various trustmark schemes and the lack of reference to existing EU initiatives regarding e-confidence and consumer protection. Despite these findings and the related recommendations, made ten years ago, very few differences can be noted. The language barrier remains a problem, with only ten out of the thirty trustmark schemes that formed part of the empirical research providing information in English (two of which only provide a one-page summary in English instead of the full website functionality in English). Of the analysed trustmarks, no single trustmark provider offers its website in more than two European languages; the ones that do offer bilingual websites are trustmarks based in countries such as Belgium or Switzerland, countries that have more than one official state language. Especially because of the ability of e-commerce to blur country borders, allowing for a wider product choice and e-consumer access to better price and quality comparisons, trustmark providers should strongly consider providing at least bilingual versions of their websites (with one version being in English) and maybe even multilingual websites.

Another reason for the difficult position of trustmarks within the EU lies in the fact that there are many trustmarks available, each with their own code of conduct, and businesses that want to be compliant with e-commerce, privacy and security requirements would have to display more than one trustmark to signal the compliance to their potential clients. The problem is that displaying too many trustmarks is likely to confuse people.[27] Websites are therefore reluctant to display trustmarks for several reasons, such as the following: they clash with the website design and colour scheme, they link to the trustmark providers' website and may thus redirect the users before they complete their purchase, or they could even seem defensive, paradoxically prompting the e-consumer to question the credibility of the website.[28] In fact, of the seven EU-based websites that appear in the top ten e-commerce websites worldwide, only two display trustmarks (the Germany-based websites *Otto.de* and *Zalando.de*); moreover, Amazon, the biggest e-retailer in Europe, does not display any trustmark whatsoever.[29]

Finally, the public perception of the meaning and value of trustmarks will also determine whether these tools will sail or sink in the long run. For instance, a reluctant—almost ironic—attitude of the public can be noted with respect to the proliferation of trustmarks and certification symbols of many types. In 2012, a German journalist wrote that there were over 500 so-called "certifying symbols" ranging from trustmarks and privacy certificates to unexpected certificates like

---

[26] De Bruin et al. 2005, p. 9.

[27] Rosner 2014, p. 24.

[28] Rule 2002, p. 107.

[29] E-Commerce News 2015.

"seniorengerecht" (n.r. fair for seniors; this symbol was launched in order to encourage supermarkets to offer services that are accessible to senior citizens, e.g. easily readable price tags).[30] The journalist concluded that, in a world where seals of approval are supposed to make order in the chaos by allowing the clear and fast identification of a product with certain qualities or attributes, "it is the seals of approval themselves that are causing chaos".[31] To conclude, it is clear that even if trustmark providers change their practices in line with the suggestions above, the public will have the last word on how privacy and data protection seals will fare in the future, and its influence cannot (and should not) be underestimated. This is why it is important for trustmark providers to design new features and characteristics with the public in mind.

6.4.2 Recent Developments

Considering the background presented above related to the different challenges of trustmarks in Europe, we turn our attention to the recent developments in the context of trustmarks in the European Union to identify potential trends.

Trustmarks have taken centre stage recently, fuelled by policy initiatives such as the US National Strategy for Trusted Identities in Cyberspace (NSTIC) and the Digital Agenda for Europe.[32] Additionally, the text of the General Data Protection Regulation specifies in Recital (100) that "[i]n order to enhance transparency and compliance with this Regulation, the establishment of certification mechanisms and data protection seals and marks should be encouraged, allowing data subjects to quickly assess the level of data protection of relevant products and services" and in Article 42 that "[t]he Member States, the supervisory authorities, the Board and the Commission shall encourage, in particular at Union level, the establishment of data protection certification mechanisms and of data protection seals and marks, for the purpose of demonstrating compliance with this Regulation of processing operations by controllers and processors". The text suggests that the use of trustmarks is likely to increase in the near-future, with more trustmarks set to enter the market for the purposes provided by the Regulation. It remains to be seen whether, in practice, such trustmarks will be useful or whether they will render the trustmark environment even less understandable to the average consumer.

In addition to the above-mentioned newcomers to the trustmark family, another type of trustmark is appearing on the horizon: the United Kingdom has announced its intention[33] to introduce a trustmark for the services part of what is known as "the sharing economy". The sharing economy is defined by the authoritative newspaper

---

[30] Der Tagesspiegel 2012.

[31] Ibid.

[32] Rosner 2014, p. 2.

[33] Financial Times 2015.

The Economist as one "in which people rent beds, cars, boats and other assets directly from each other, co-ordinated via the internet."[34] The UK's initiative to introduce a trustmark for such services will undoubtedly contribute to raising awareness of the concept of trustmark—but again, the actual effect of this initiative remains to be seen in practice.

With all the new types of trustmarks trying to win market share and influence, it is perhaps a suitable moment to remember that trustmarks were initially launched for a simple, straightforward purpose—to build trust, increase user confidence in making online purchases and thus contribute to the growth of e-commerce. However, whilst the European e-commerce environment grew over time, it is uncertain how much this growth can be attributed to the use of trustmarks and how much to other factors, such as the improvement of internet access and the proliferation of the modern on-the-go lifestyle, which makes consumers reach for the computer to quickly purchase items. Given the lack of a tool to measure the performance of trustmarks, providers have found it difficult to tailor the trustmarks to the needs of the e-consumers.

6.5 The Need for a Yardstick to Determine the Impact of Trustmarks

Research has found that "the heterogeneity of the trustmark landscape makes it difficult to determine the importance of the characteristics of trustmarks for establishing trust."[35] The fragmentation and variety of the trustmark landscape requires an in-depth analysis of their features to identify the main points that need to be addressed to ensure a better experience for customers and a heightened level of awareness of trustmarks in general. In the report cited above, researchers conducted a survey to identify the views of the stakeholders on the value of trustmarks for web-shops and for consumers, respectively.[36] The stakeholders addressed were trade associations, trustmark providers and consumer associations. Overall, the stakeholders considered the verification of the web-shop's reputation and the verification of the quality of the sales process to be the most important characteristics of trustmarks.

Unsurprisingly, however, the method of asking stakeholders to evaluate trustmark characteristics according to a set list of criteria resulted in a subjective view in the case of each stakeholder, in accordance with the pursued interests. This exercise did not provide an accurate, objective overview on the trustmark landscape because of the distorted results. For instance, trustmark providers value the "trustmark attributes" higher than the trade associations—this is because the trustmark attributes are both their selling points and the factors that differentiate them from the

---

[34] The Economist 2013.

[35] Building Digital Confidence in Europe 2012, p. 40.

[36] Building Digital Confidence in Europe 2012, pp. 65–75.

competition. However, consumers do not attach such high value to trustmark attributes, again raising the issue of lack of information combined with lack of interest. At the same time, industry associations attach less importance than the consumer organisations to the verification and quality of the dispute resolution process, the verification and assurance of the technical security of the connection, and the verification of the quality of the sales process—this is not surprising, given that industry associations work together specifically to supervise these issues.

The expectations of the stakeholders, taken separately, were different from the expectations of the other stakeholders, and quite one-sided. It can therefore be concluded that a different approach is needed to measure the value of trustmarks in an objective manner. The most appropriate solution is to establish a yardstick by which to assess different trustmarks and how they measure up against each other, based on a list of specific criteria. Developing an objective tool to measure the impact of trustmarks and to compare the features is a solution-based approach that will result in a streamlined, coherent, objective and focused outcome.

One such example of a yardstick was introduced by one of the authors in his book "Trustmarks in E-Commerce".[37] The proposed yardstick consists of the following elements, which were selected to ensure a trustworthy assessment: the independence of the trustmark provider, the impartiality in the auditing process, the active monitoring of the certificate owner's practice, the enforcement power of the trustmark provider and the accountability of the same. These elements have been considered in the analysis of the Terms and Conditions of selected trustmark providers, which is carried out from practical perspective and laid out in Sect. 6.7 of this chapter. The independence of the trustmark provider is addressed in Sects. 6.7.2 and 6.7.3, which analyse the governance of the trustmark scheme and the strictness of the requirements for joining. The impartiality in the auditing process, the active monitoring and enforcement of the code of conduct are discussed in Sects. 6.7.4 and 6.7.5, which address the issues around compliance monitoring and the actions taken for non-compliance. Finally, the liability of trustmark providers is reflected in Sect. 6.7.6, which provides insight into the disclaimers of liability that are usually utilised by trustmark providers. This structure was adopted it provides the reader with a new approach to the previously developed yardstick, demonstrating how such a tool can be used in different ways to objectively assess and compare trustmark providers and their practices.

6.6 Reconciling Stakeholder Expectations

To determine the possible ways to reconcile stakeholders' expectations, it is useful to look at the story of the *Which? Web Trader (W?WT)* scheme, launched by the UK Consumer's Association as the predecessor of the trustmark as we know it

---

[37] Balboni 2009, p. 53.

today. When it launched in 2001, its self-stated purpose was to promote consumer confidence in on-line shopping. It aimed at achieving this through the creation of an eighteen-point voluntary code of good practice, which traders had to sign and respect. Once they obtained the W?WT seal of approval, the traders were then subject to random checks in to ensure they were, in practice, complying with the requirements of the code of conduct. Whilst the scheme was well thought-out and seemed to perform well (it resolved more than 2000 disputes on behalf of e-consumers),[38] it closed after only three and a half years because it was too costly to run. The story of the W?WT scheme foreshadowed some of the problems that trustmark providers encounter today, such as the problem of pitching for resources whilst remaining an impartial player on the market.

To provide a good service, trustmark providers need resources (financial and otherwise). To obtain resources, they need to either be subsidised by a govern-mental program, sponsored by private sponsors or they need to raise the money themselves. The most frequently encountered situation is that trustmark providers raise their own capital, to enable them to run the scheme, by offering the seal in exchange for a recurring membership fee to different web-shops. Currently, membership fees for the thirty analysed trustmark schemes range from roughly 100 Euro per year to more than 2000 Euro, depending on the trustmark-providing organisation and on the size of the company requesting a trustmark and the country of origin. The problem is that the subscribers expect to be able to quantify the benefits of joining a trustmark scheme in monetary form (return on investment or ROI), especially if that same trustmark scheme also requires the subscriber to undergo complex procedures and periodic checks to retain the right to display the seal.

Trustmark providers are therefore in the position of having to convince web-shop owners that the trustmark not only gives peace of mind to the e-consumers, but also that it makes them purchase more products more frequently. As a result, trustmark providers have been refocusing their sales proposition by moving towards business-oriented goals, through slogans such as: "if you use our trustmark, you will have more customers" or "if you purchase this certificate, your sales will increase".[39] The direct consequence is that the initial purpose of the trustmark, to boost the confidence of e-consumers and enhance e-commerce, is fading in favour of secondary advantages provided by trustmarks, such as increased web traffic or a more engaged consumer base. This phenomenon could result in the trustmark losing its core value as a compliance tool, thus risking becoming an advertising, or marketing gimmick.[40]

The main problem lies in how trustmarks are perceived by e-consumers and by web-shop owners. If there is a lack of alignment of perceptions, the trustmark will likely fail its mission as a tool that bridges the virtual gap between web-shop

---

[38] Out-Law.com, at http://www.out-law.com/page-3223. Accessed 26 April 2016.

[39] More information on this topic can be found in Sect. 6.7.2 of this chapter.

[40] See Balboni 2009, pp. 33ss.

owners and e-consumers. From the perspective of the web-shop owners who perceive trustmarks as "add-ons" meant to enhance web traffic or to bring in new clients deforms the primary meaning of the schemes and causes confusion about the value and purpose of web seals. On the other hand, from the perspective of e-consumers, seeing trustmarks as tools that guarantee 100% web safety is not realistic, and, given the characteristics of the internet, it would not be very smart to rely exclusively on the presence of a trustmark to make a purchasing decision. Therefore, by staggering the expectations of web-shop owners and e-consumers, an alignment of perception could be achieved, which could lead to an improved understanding of the trustmark concept and to a better use of it as a tool.

The most reasonable and straightforward way to reconcile the expectations of web-shop owners with the ones of e-consumers is to establish the view that web seals are symbols of the effort and determination of a web-shop owner to comply with industry standards. This interpretation would strike the right balance between rewarding the web-shop owners who make a conscious effort of following a code of conduct set out by a trustmark provider, and inspiring trust on the side of e-consumers. Another important aspect to consider is that consumers should be aware that trustmarks, whilst certainly helpful, are not meant to replace good judgment and autonomous decision-making. Responsibility should be shared in case of an unforeseen mistake or problem related to a purchase.

The principle of accountability is also of significant importance. Trustmark providers need to be accountable to be taken seriously by web-shop owners and consumers alike, otherwise they are providing a service that makes promises with no warranties. Web-shop owners also need to be held accountable regarding their implementation of the code of conduct or trustmark requirements, preferably by means of a mechanism of recurring auditing to keep track of their compliance status and by displaying the time stamp of the most recent successfully passed audit. Finally, consumers should be accountable for their purchase choices, in the sense that they should look at the trustmark as a positive sign showing the compliance of a website, but they should remain wary of potential fake displays of trustmarks, unusual activity of the visited website, or browser warnings.

Once trustmarks are perceived as compliance tools, rather than as marketing tools that can increase sales, they become objectively valuable. Trustmarks would be similar to medals won in sporting competitions: they would attest that a website had made a conscious effort to be compliant and that, at a specific point in time, it respected all the requirements of the code of conduct, making it very likely (but not 100% guaranteed) that it has maintained the same practices and is still compliant. This is comparable to the case of a runner or a swimmer who obtained a medal: the medal represents an indication of the contestant's dedication and hard work, but it should not represent a burden for the contestant to always give the same level of performance regardless of the external circumstances.

Positioning trustmarks as compliance tools may be beneficial not only for consumers, who would have a clear picture of what they can expect from websites that display a trustmark, but also for the websites themselves, that will not be held at unrealistically high standards. In addition (and pursuing the sporting metaphor), repeating the verification of the compliance at recurring points in time and in special circumstances, for instance in the event of significant legal or technical changes, is strongly recommended. As mentioned above, displaying a time stamp of the last compliance check would be a useful incentive in this case, as it would enable consumers to know when the last time was that the web-shop was "tested and approved" for compliance. For instance, in case of legal changes, the consumer would know whether the seal was awarded according to the old or the new regulation. This argument is particularly convincing given the recent Safe Harbor decision, which invalidated the data transfers from the EU to the US on the basis of the Decision 2000/520/EC.[41] In this case, seeing a website display a seal of approval alongside a time stamp dated prior to the Safe Harbor decision would mean that the website was checked prior to the legal changes and may no longer be compliant. On the other hand, seeing a more recent timestamp would enable the averagely informed consumers to draw the conclusion that the website had adapted its procedures to the new laws.

In conclusion, reconciling stakeholder expectations would be beneficial for streamlining and harmonising the concept of trustmark itself, for example by encouraging the perception of trustmarks as awards given for compliance, but not as the only indicator on which to base a purchasing decision. Organising informational campaigns to achieve this would be a good starting point and would pave the way for the introduction of more specific and fine-tuned trustmark schemes. The introduction of regular checks and time stamps showing the most recent verified compliance would contribute to creating e-confidence. Most importantly, the suggested perception would solve the problem of risk allocation between stakeholders, by encouraging each to bear a share of the responsibility, and to actively work towards compliance and mitigation of cyber threats.

6.7 Analysis of the Terms & Conditions of EU-Based Trustmark Schemes

This section deals with trustmarks from a legal perspective. To assess the advantages and challenges that trustmarks face, this section focuses on the different trustmark schemes that are active in the EU. Since the authors are legal professionals based in the EU, the focus of this chapter has been specifically put on European trustmark practices, especially in the light of the enactment of the new Regulation 2016/679, whose Article 42 creates a significant opportunity for trustmarks to gain importance. It has therefore been considered useful to analyse the various practices of the current trustmark providers, to draw the relevant conclusions regarding the potential areas for improvement. With the new Regulation, it is

---

[41] Court of Justice of The European Union 2015 at http://curia.europa.eu/jcms/upload/docs/application/pdf/2015-10/cp150117en.pdf. Accessed 26 April 2016.

envisaged that trustmarks will become an ever-more valuable and effective tool for consumers, which is why there is no time like the present to conduct this analysis. For the purposes of this chapter, only the trustmarks that provide a website in English, German, French, Spanish, Italian or Romanian have been taken into consideration as examples.

The full list of the trustmark schemes that were considered for this research includes the following: EuroPriSe (Schleswig Holstein/Germany), EHI Geprüfter Online Shop (Euro-label group, Germany), Güte Zeichen (Austria), Euro-label "Sicher Einkaufen" (Austria), BeCommerce (Belgium), Confianza Online (Spain), Swiss Online Garantie VSV (Switzerland), EMOTA (Europe-wide 'umbrella' trustmark), SafeBuy (United Kingdom), TÜVSÜD Safer Shopping (Germany), TrustedShops (Germany).

6.7.1   Scope and Methodology

The purpose of this empirical research was to analyse the various aspects of trustmarks in practice. The research was conducted with the aim of identifying similarities and differences between the various schemes, whilst at the same time evaluating whether a common, harmonised and coherent "trustmark model" can be identified. The research is structured around the following five main questions, which have been developed starting from the yardstick discussed in Sect. 6.5 above.

- How does the governance scheme of the various trustmark organisations and the way they are marketed to the public affect their independence?
- How impartial are the various trustmark providers in assessing the requirements for joining a trustmark scheme and in determining a specific procedure for joining, based on strict criteria?
- Is active compliance monitoring in place, and if so, how often is it undertaken and based on what criteria?
- How, and to what extent, does a trustmark organisation enforce its code of conduct and what actions are taken by the trustmark providers in case a web-shop does not comply with the code of conduct? Is there a clear list of sanctions for specific offences or are trustmark providers being too lenient?
- How accountable are trustmark providers, to what extent do they assume liability and what is included in the disclaimers?

6.7.2   How Does the Governance Scheme of the Various Trustmark Organisations and the Way They Are Marketed to the Public Affect Their Independence?

Only a very small percentage of trustmark schemes are government-owned. An example of such a trustmark is *eShop* in Malta. Previously *EuroPriSe* in Germany, which was initiated by the federal state of Schleswig Holstein, was government-owned but has since been privatised. *EuroPriSe* stands for European Privacy Seal and is intended to be an overarching trustmark scheme for security and privacy compliance. By studying the *EuroPriSe* fact sheet that is available for download from the website, one thing that jumps to the eye is the use of marketing advantage as a selling tool, written in bold alongside "trust": "[…] and at the same time provides a marketing advantage to manufacturers and vendors of privacy respecting goods and services".[42] The same phenomenon can be noted on the website of the *SafeBuy* trustmark where website owners are advised that the use of the trustmark will help them "maximise pending orders, turning them into sales". Furthermore, the website even directly states that "the risk is non-existent", implying that the display of a trustmark on a website is a benefits-only, low-responsibility task. Similarly, *Trusted Shops* uses the keywords "traffic", "conversion" and "building your customer base" to entice web-shop owners to purchase a subscription. There is no mention of the need to comply with the Quality Criteria on the http://business.trustedshops.de/ homepage. The approach of marketing the trustmark as a tool for increasing business, rather than focusing on the compliance with a code of conduct or with specific criteria, is quite problematic. There is a risk of downplaying the importance of compliance with a scheme and of underestimating the need of providing a safe shopping environment.

On the other hand, the *TÜV SÜD Safer Shopping* trustmark scheme, for instance, emphasises the value that the trustmark adds through its compliance mechanism, by using slogans such as "Establish trust with certified safety" or "Create active trust". The use of the trustmark as a marketing tool was also mentioned (the website suggests "an increase in turnover due to reduced order cancellations") but in this case its role was significantly more restrained, in favour of the security and privacy compliance aspects. The *EHI* trustmark, provided by the EHI Retail Institute also approaches the matter from a security and compliance perspective, marketing its auditing procedure, know-how and certification criteria instead. The use of the trustmark as a "marketing tool" that promises more conversions takes the secondary place. This is the case of the Austrian trustmark *Österreichisches E-Commerce-Gütezeichen*, which is awarded to companies that "distinguish themselves through serious business transactions and customer friendliness that extends beyond the minimum statutory requirements" (according to its own code of conduct).[43] This trustmark provider, the *Association for the development of customer-friendly internet practices*, does not mention the secondary marketing advantages that could potentially be gained by the adherence to the trustmark scheme, focusing instead on the certification procedure and the compliance aspects.

This first look at the trustmark providers reveals that for the most part industry organisations emphasise the value of trustmarks as a compliance tool, helping

---

[42] See https://www.european-privacy-seal.eu/AppFile/GetFile/99c44bed-802e-41ef-9a7e-8c77d18 76bc3. Accessed 26 April 2016.

[43] See https://www.guetezeichen.at/unternehmen/kriterien/. Accessed 26 April 2016.

web-shops align themselves with the security/privacy requirements of the code of conduct, whereas private companies and government organisations stress the value of trustmarks both in demonstrating compliance and as a way to increase sales and convert pending orders into confirmed ones. However, we note that this division in marketing trustmarks applies as a general rule, but there are also exceptions—TÜV SÜD, for instance, is a private company that emphasises the compliance aspect. Nevertheless, the main problem with this difference in approach is that the concept of trustmark is not consistent, which makes it difficult for a web-shop owner to decide which trustmark to use and at the same time, it is difficult for the average consumer to decisively rely on a specific trustmark. Another issue is that this approach undermines the need for compliance in the first place—the reader should note that the privacy and security requirements presented by many trustmarks are not unusually high, though they are (or should be) the standard for every online shop. By marketing the tool in this way an unclear and incoherent message about the significance of the trustmark is sent to consumers and web-shop owners. More consistency would ensure that the trustmarks are perceived as a valuable and reliable tool.

6.7.3   How Impartial Are the Various Trustmark Providers in Assessing the Requirements for Joining a Trustmark Scheme and What Is the Procedure to Join Based on Strict Criterion Place?

The second part of the assessment relates to the procedure to join or participate in the trustmark scheme. To be reliable, a trustmark should be awarded only when the business requesting it fully complies with the set of requirements exhibited by the trustmark provider. The set of criteria should represent at least the minimum business standards expected from a web-shop owner. If these two requirements are not respected, then the award of the trustmark loses relevance and the display of the trustmark on a webpage does not provide any real guarantee to the potential customer.

From the empirical research conducted, we note that there is a significant difference in the joining procedure. Some trustmark providers have a very strict joining procedure (such as *EuroPriSe*, which has a fifty-nine-page PDF containing the criteria for joining and the joining procedure).[44] Other trustmark organisations require only a few steps before the trader can display a trustmark on their website, such as in the case of *BeCommerce*, where the web trader can submit all the information for accreditation via the website. Some trustmarks have no apparent steps or procedures that must be completed before being awarded, requiring instead only payment of a fee, such as *SafeBuy UK*.

---

[44] See https://www.european-privacy-seal.eu/EPS-en/Criteria. Accessed 26 April 2016.

Amongst the trustmark schemes with detailed, step-by-step joining procedures is the *EHI* trustmark. It has a five-step process in place before it approves a member and gives it the right to display the web seal: after a trader requests a trustmark, *EHI* carries out an assessment of the online shop, makes recommendations, helps the trader implement them and only at the end of the process, awards the trustmark. The pricing starts at 62,50 Euro per month and varies depending on the trader's size (established by annual turnover) up to 2800,00 Euro per year. The assessment of the e-shop includes a verification of the legal texts (Privacy Policy, Terms of Use, information that the shop is required by law to provide the customers with) and an assessment of the product descriptions, the pre- and post-contractual obligations of each contracting party and the use of tracking tools such as Google Analytics.

Similarly, the *TÜV SÜD* trustmark provides potential applicants for the web seal with a ten-page document of requirements that the organisation needs to comply with prior to being awarded the trustmark.[45] The document includes provisions regarding organisational requirements, data security, data protection and online processes. The price for the compliance procedure and award of the trustmark is available upon request and allegedly varies from 3,000 to 30,000 Euro per year.

Other trustmark schemes, however, do not offer a strong list of well-developed criteria and certify shops without asking for too much information—arguably, because it makes the process easier and brings in more clients, therefore is a (more) profitable business model. For instance, *SafeBuy* only requires five minutes of a trader's time—or less, if he or she manages to fill in their credit card details faster, since upfront payment appears to be the only requirement. There is a Code of Practice on the website, however the link is not easy to find and throughout the subscription process there is no indication of an obligation to respect it.[46] The Code of Practice seems more like an afterthought than a requirement. The trustmark is awarded instantly for a sixty-day trial, after which it is renewed automatically at the price of 18.99 British Pounds/month + VAT or 199.00 British Pounds + VAT annually.

Similarly, the Romanian *Trusted.ro* trustmark is awarded upon payment of 120.00 Euro + VAT fee (per year), based on the self-assessment of the web traders and their declaration that they comply with the criteria established by the provider.[47] However, as opposed to *SafeBuy*, *Trusted.ro* includes a term in their contract with the trader that requires performing at least one review of the compliance with the certification criteria within the first seven months after the award of the trustmark. While compliance monitoring and auditing will be addressed at large in the following section, it is highlighted here to show that there is some action taken by the provider to minimise instances where a web trader might perform an incorrect self-assessment, whether intentionally or by mistake.

---

[45] See https://www.safer-shopping.de/uploads/PDF/Requirements_Shopsb2c.pdf. Accessed 26 April 2016.

[46] See http://care.safebuy.org.uk/code-of-practice/. Accessed 26 April 2016.

[47] See https://www.trusted.ro/wp-content/uploads/2014/10/Standarde_Trusted_ro_oct2014.pdf [ROMANIAN]. Accessed 26 April 2016.

6.7.4   Is Active Compliance Monitoring in Place, and If So, How Often Is It Undertaken and Based on What Criteria?

A crucial aspect for the good functioning of trustmarks is how often the certified shops are assessed for compliance. Given the speed of growth of online businesses and of cyber threats alike, any certification should be constantly updated and reviewed to ensure that it remains relevant. As suggested above, some trustmark providers do not conduct an assessment of a web shop prior to awarding the badge (for instance, *SafeBuy* and *Trusted.ro*) which means that a trustmark may be displayed on a webpage even in cases where the web trader does not (fully) comply with the scheme. This has two negative consequences: firstly, consumers unwittingly rely on the trustmark displayed on the webpage and may unwillingly become victims of online fraud; secondly, this practice could lower the relevance of trustmarks in general because very few consumers have time to research each single trustmark to learn the differences between them, and therefore their general idea of what a trustmark is would be seriously affected due to even just one negative experience.

Web-shops should be monitored and/or audited regularly because e-commerce is a constantly changing environment, and some business decisions may affect the rights of the consumers or may significantly change the business model. For example, a look through the list of members of the *SafeBuy* scheme reveals that several web-shops are currently closed or sell other goods or services than the ones they have been certified for, thus suggesting that the certification is unreliable (for example, http://www.luxurybeautyshop.co.uk/ which was awarded Accreditation nr. 1110101, was certified for the sale of fragrances and beauty products but instead redirects to a webpage selling tickets for London theatre shows. This proves that regular monitoring and compliance is highly important to ensure that trustmarks are reliable always).

Other trustmark schemes, such as *EuroPriSe,* provide a very clear overview of the trustmark certification of each of its members, including details about when the certificate was awarded (together with a PDF version of it), a public report, the dates of scheduled recertification, a description and summary of the activities of the website or product, as well as warnings in case of specific issues. The *EuroPriSe* trustmark expires after two years, after which recertification is required. Similarly, the *Handelsverband Austria* trustmark is only awarded for a period of twelve months, after which a recertification procedure is undertaken. All members of the EMOTA scheme (Safeshops.be, EPAM Greece, bevh/EHI Geprüfter online Shop, Webshop Keurmerk, Trygg e-Handel, ceneje.si, Swiss Online Garantie VSV) are bound by the requirement of EMOTA to review the certification minimum once per year and, in exceptional circumstances, random checks are carried out.

Despite very few exceptions, trustmarks offer yearly reviews. This is positive because they incentivise the web trader to make an active effort to be compliant to be able to display the web seals. However, annual reviews should be supplemented by random checks, which would ensure that web-shop owners endeavour to be fully compliant year-round, instead of once a year, and that there is an awareness of the importance of continued compliance. In addition, random checks would enable the identification of potential non-compliance early on, reducing the risk of displaying a trustmark on a non-compliant website for an extended period. Random checks would also be a good way to make sure that websites that were certified in the past continue to be compliant with the requirements of the scheme always, even when changing business type or model (as per the example above).

6.7.5 How, and to What Extent, Does a Trustmark Organisation Enforce Its Code of Conduct and What Actions Are Taken by the Trustmark Providers in the Case of a Web Shop Not Complying with the Code of Conduct? Is There a Clear List of Sanctions for Specific Offences or Are Trustmark Providers Being Too Lenient?

The empirical research conducted revealed that most trustmark providers do not have a specific procedure in place for sanctions in case of non-compliance with the specific code of conduct. This is very likely as most subscriptions are renewable on a yearly or two-year basis and each renewal means the payment of another fee by the web-shop to the trustmark provider. It is reasonable to infer that trustmark providers prefer to wait until the point of review (once a year, in most cases) and then proceed to identify and correct any non-compliances, instead of pointing them out promptly and removing the trader from its list of approved websites, thus ending a business relationship.[48]

EMOTA very vaguely states that it will "address any relevant issues with the trader, who will need to correct them promptly" and that "The Trust Mark *can* be withdrawn if the trader does not comply with the code of conduct or in the case of insolvency". However, it is not clear what "promptly means" or what is supposed to happen before the trustmark is withdrawn (i.e., how many strikes before a trader is out). Some trustmark providers do not indicate the specific circumstances under which their trustmark may be withdrawn—take *EuroPrise*, for example. Others refer to the possibility of withdrawing the right to use a web seal, however not for breach but in the case of lack of payment on time—see *Be Commerce*'s Code de Conduite, Article 4 *(French version only)*.[49]

---

[48] Balboni 2009, p. 54.

[49] See https://www.becommerce.be/files/Code_de_conduite_du_Label_de_Qualite_BeCommerce.pdf [French]. Accessed 26 April 2016.

On the contrary, there are some trustmark providers that tackle the issue in an appropriate manner. A very good example is that of *EHI Geprüfter Online Shop*, which specifies that the right of the web-shop owner to display the trustmark may be interrupted if the owner breaches the Code of Conduct "repeatedly, in an on-going manner or substantially", if customer complaints are not dealt with promptly and in an appropriate manner, if the payment of the fee is delayed by over thirty days, or if the data related to the revenue turns out to be untrue or if the web-shop becomes insolvent—see *§ 9 Vertragsdauer/-kündigung und Entzug des Siegels (duration of the contract, termination and withdrawal of the seal)*.[50] Similarly, *TÜV SÜD* discusses the possibility of withdrawal of the trustmark in its Testing and Certification Regulations at point A-1.2: "If the requirements are not fulfilled within the defined deadlines, the certificate will be deemed withdrawn on expiry of said deadlines and will have to be returned by the certificate holder to the issuing TSC without delay".[51]

It is very important that traders are aware not only of the conditions under which they may be awarded a trustmark, but also of the conditions in which a trustmark may be revoked. One reason for this is the need for contractual certainty—if they know what may provoke the withdrawal, they may pay more attention to those issues and endeavour to address them in a timely manner. The second reason is that there needs to be a liability associated with a breach of the right to display the trustmark, otherwise there would be little incentive to try and uphold the terms of the code of conduct, since waiting for the review would mean that the trustmark organisation identifies and fixes the non-compliance. Being strict about instances of non-compliance would be a further positive step for trustmark organisations towards the goal of establishing a coherent, valuable and reliable concept of trustmark.

6.7.6 Liability and Disclaimers

Finally, the last aspect analysed (but by no means the least important) is the issue of liability of trustmark providers and of the related disclaimers that are often introduced in the Terms and Conditions to limit the liability of trustmark providers as much as possible.

Each trustmark analysed has explicitly limited its liability "to the highest extent permitted by law". This approach is, in general, understandable from a business perspective. However, in the business of "trust", reliable and explicit guarantees should be given to consumers to enable them to rely on the certifications issued by a

---

[50] See https://ehi-siegel.de/shopbetreiber/ehi-siegel/pruef-kriterien-bedingungen/teilnahmebedingungen/ [German]. Accessed 26 April 2016.

[51] See https://www.safer-shopping.de/uploads/PDF/TestingCertRegulations.pdf. Accessed 26 April 2016.

specific trustmark provider. Otherwise, how can consumers trust a trustmark provider that certifies that a specific shop is safe to use, when the trustmark provider has much to gain (in terms of clients and profits) but does not stand to lose anything through the certification?

In other words, trustmark providers should not be able to certify web-shops and thus induce consumers to enter into commercial contracts, but then refuse any responsibility connected with the certification and impose instead all liability on the consumers themselves. This is where the concept of warranted trust comes into play: for trust to be warranted (i.e., "justified", "well-grounded" and "plausible"),[52] the trust or and the trustee need to balance out the advantages and the liabilities, otherwise the imbalance creates a lack of trust that is the exact opposite from what was intended."[53]

6.7.7 Recurring Issues

From a legal perspective, three recurring problems can be identified in the current trustmarks scheme. First, the lack of regulatory action means that the market is highly fragmented and each trustmark provider functions based on its own rules. This makes it difficult for e-consumers to trust the notion of 'trustmark', as what a trustmark is cannot be clearly defined and is left to depend on the circumstances, varying according to each provider. Second, a phenomenon of 'scope creep' in relation to trust marks can be identified. Whereas the original purpose of a trustmark was to reassure customers that the web-shop displaying its badge was reliable, this has now expanded to include other aims, such as guaranteeing the web-shop owner more visibility or promising to increase sales. Third, the issue of accountability of trustmark providers towards e-consumers who make a purchase while relying on the trustmark requires drawing a fine line between the responsibility of the trustmark provider in certifying a website and the level of risk inherent in any transaction.

Resolving these issues is highly recommended and finding the appropriate solution would lead to a more coherent trustmark landscape. These aspects should be considered when creating a new trustmark scheme or refining an existing one. Additionally, given the importance of the public perception of trustmarks, educational campaigns informing the public about the meaning and function of trustmarks would help create the positive image that trustmarks need to gain importance and stay relevant in the fast-paced, ever-changing e-market.

---

[52] Stanford Encyclopaedia of Philosophy entry, available at http://plato.stanford.edu/entries/trust/. Accessed 26 April 2016.

[53] Balboni 2009, pp. 207ss.

6.8 Conclusions

The purpose of this chapter was to analyse the challenges and controversies of trustmarks by tackling the various issues from a theoretical point of view, analysing various academic resources and surveys and from a practical perspective through empirical research into the practices of eleven EU-based trustmark providers (whose webpages were in languages that were accessible to the authors) of the thirty schemes based in the EU that were identified in total. This was done with a view to inform the future development of privacy and data protection seals.

The chapter started out by setting the scene and reviewing the role of trustmarks in e-commerce. Trustmarks can be valuable tools for increasing consumer confidence in e-commerce, but for this to happen in practice, trustmarks need to reach critical mass and to stimulate awareness. Currently, there are still practical and regulatory barriers which impede the trustmark from gaining momentum. One way of breaking these barriers could be, for instance, by means of a public authority supporting or endorsing a trustmark scheme and by introducing marketing and informational campaigns containing clear, accessible and simple explanations. Businesses should be encouraged to subscribe to trustmark schemes and consumers should be educated about what each web seals signifies.

The chapter continued with the section on the characteristics and functions of trustmarks. Trustmarks have the capacity to make the unknown seem familiar, thus stimulating e-consumers to actively participate in e-commerce. Problems arise, though, if the stakeholder triangle (e-consumer, e-trader and trustmark provider) falls out of balance. The main issue is that each stakeholder has a subjective view of what the trustmark is; this view includes the idea that the responsibility is to be borne by the other players, which is not realistic. Trustmarks should be neither merchant-centric nor consumer-centric; instead, a neutral model should be established whereby trustmarks are viewed as compliance tools, rather than marketing, sales or commercially-focused tools. A suggested approach is treating trustmarks as "medals" certifying the effort of web traders, without necessarily meaning that they provide the ultimate guarantee that the environment is completely secure; consumers should make autonomous decisions of purchase, assessing all factors involved, including but not limited to trustmarks. In the context of the European Union, the lack of European sensitivity along with the heterogeneity of the trustmark environment are the two main problems. If trustmarks are to become established as reliable tools, public perception is very important; solving the two problems is likely to contribute to an improved public perception of what trustmarks are and what they do. Greater clarity, more multilingual resources and more information about each web seal award (such as the time stamp of the first and/or most recent certification) would help in this respect. Building awareness in a certain marketplace or focusing on a specific target market may help trustmark providers establish a relevant trustmark for a specific area of e-commerce. Trustmark providers could also attempt to have an open dialogue with each other to streamline the fragmented market and convey a coherent image of the "trustmark as a tool".

The chapter established the need for a yardstick to objectively measure the impact of individual trustmarks within the e-commerce market and against each other. This method was used in Sect. 6.7 of the chapter, where the various aspects of the different trustmarks were discussed based on criteria such as joining requirements, marketing strategy, governance scheme, actions in case of non-compliance and trustmark providers' liability. The empirical research led to a series of important, practical and business-oriented conclusions. First, trustmarks are not marketed consistently, since the various providers use opposing qualities as selling points (compliance versus customer generation); an incorrect message about the significance and utility of trustmarks is being sent to consumers which hurts the public perception of trustmarks in the long run. More consistency is recommended in this respect. Second, trustmark application/subscription procedures range from very simple (filling in credit card details for the subscription) to very complex (five step procedures, 50-page Codes of Conduct etc.). Compliance monitoring also differs from provider to provider, with some trustmark organisations performing yearly checks and others not even conducting an initial assessment prior to the award of the web seal. The introduction of random checks would improve the situation, as it would allow non-conformities to be identified early on and especially in cases where traders can join based on self-assessment only. Of course, the identified non-conformities should be sanctioned or at least promptly addressed and rectified, otherwise the reliability of web seals is questionable. The last part of the research identified the basis for the liability of trustmark providers in cases of transactions gone wrong due to a fault attributable to them.

Finally, the chapter summarises the findings and analysed the three main controversies from a legal perspective, concluding that regulatory action should be taken for the purposes of harmonising trustmark schemes and, at the same time, to raise awareness. Trustmarks should be shielded from the 'scope creep' phenomenon and should instead focus on their main function. Furthermore, the principle of accountability should be enshrined in the relationship between the stakeholders, to maximise the value that society can obtain from trustmarks.

If these recommendations are followed, trustmarks will be able to graduate from their current fragmented, unclear status and become the reliable e-commerce companions they were created to be. However, if no significant changes are made regarding the approach and perception of the trustmarks, these signs will succumb to the pressure exerted by the controversies and challenges surrounding them and will have the fate of the floppy disk or CD-ROM—they will become obsolete. One can only hope that they will follow the first path, but it remains to be seen how they develop, especially following the introduction of the General Data Protection Regulation and in general, the heightened interest in privacy and protection of personal data.

References

Balboni P (2009) Trustmarks in E-Commerce. The Value of Web Seals and the Liability of their Providers. TMC Asser Press, The Hague

BeCommerce.Be (2013) Code de Conduite du Label de Qualité BeCommerce pour la Vente a Distance. https://www.becommerce.be/files/Code_de_conduite_du_Label_de_Qualite_BeCommerce.pdf. Accessed 26 April 2016

Cortés P (2011) Online Dispute Resolution for Consumers in the European Union. Routledge, Abingdon

Court of Justice of the European Union (2015) The Court of Justice declares that the Commission's US Safe Harbour Decision is invalid. http://curia.europa.eu/jcms/upload/docs/application/pdf/2015-10/cp150117en.pdf. Accessed on 27 April 2016

De Bruin R, Keuleers E, Lazaro C, Poullet Y, Viersma M (2005) Analysis and definition of common characteristics of trustmarks and web seals in the European Union – Final Report. Available at http://www.crid.be/pdf/public/5026.pdf. Accessed 26 April 2016

E-Commerce News (2015) E-Commerce in Europe. http://ecommercenews.eu/ecommerce-per-country/ecommerce-in-europe/#stores. Accessed 26 April 2016

E-Consultancy (2011) Which e-commerce trustmarks are most effective? https://econsultancy.com/blog/7941-which-e-commerce-trustmarks-are-most-effective/. Accessed 26 April 2016

EHI Geprüfter Online Shop (2016) Teilnahmebedingungen EHI Geprüfter Online-Shop. https://ehi-siegel.de/shopbetreiber/ehi-siegel/pruef-kriterien-bedingungen/teilnahmebedingungen/. Accessed 26 April 2016

EMOTA Website (2016) A pan-European Network of E-Commerce Trustmarks. http://www.emota.eu/#!ecommercetrustmark/c1jas. Accessed 26 April 2016

EUR-Lex (2016) Proposal for a REGULATION OF THE EUROPEAN PARLIAMENT AND OF THE COUNCIL on the protection of individuals with regard to the processing of personal data and on the free movement of such data (General Data Protection Regulation). http://eur-lex.europa.eu/legal-content/EN/TXT/?uri=CELEX%3A52012PC0011. Accessed 26 April 2016

European Consumer Centres Network (2013) Trustmarks Report: "Can I trust the trustmark?" http://ec.europa.eu/dgs/health_food-safety/information_sources/docs/trust_mark_report_2013_en.pdf. Accessed 26 April 2016

European Consumer Centres Network (2011) Online Cross-Border Mystery Shopping – State of the E-Union. http://dokumenter.forbrug.dk/forbrugereuropa/onlinecrossbordermysteryshopping/web.pdf. Accessed 26 April 2016

European Union Committee on Online Platforms and the Digital Single Market (2016) 10th Report of Session 2015-16, HL Paper 129. http://www.publications.parliament.uk/pa/ld201516/ldselect/ldeucom/129/12902.htm. Accessed 26 April 2016

EuroPriSe (2011) Certification Criteria. https://www.european-privacy-seal.eu/EPS-en/Criteria. Accessed 26 April 2016

EuroPriSe (2014) Fact Sheet. https://www.european-privacy-seal.eu/AppFile/GetFile/99c44bed-802e-41ef-9a7e-8c77d1876bc3. Accessed April 2016

Eurostat – statistics explained (2015) E-commerce statistics. http://ec.europa.eu/eurostat/statistics-explained/index.php/E-commerce_statistics. Accessed 26 April 2016

Financial Times (2015) UK to create trustmark for app businesses in 'sharing economy'. http://www.ft.com/cms/s/0/36562c48-2ef8-11e5-8873-775ba7c2ea3d.html#axzz3zbHkLBpl. Accessed 26 April 2016

Mayer RC, Davis JH, Schoorman F (1995) An integrative model of organizational trust, Academy of Management Review Vol. 20, No. 3 (July 1995), pp. 709–734

OECD Digital Economy Papers (2013) No. 216: Empowering and Protecting Consumers in the Internet Economy. http://www.oecd-ilibrary.org/docserver/download/5k4c6tbcvvq2.pdf?

expires=1456165455&id=id&accname=guest&checksum=CF92EDB12A274334C90DF6CABC 2FFF2E. Accessed 26 April 2016

Österreichisches E-Commerce-Gütezeichen (2014) Kriterien des Österreichischen E-Commerce-Gütezeichen https://www.guetezeichen.at/unternehmen/kriterien/. Accessed 26 April 2016

Out-Law.com (2003) Which? Web Trader scheme to close due to costs. http://www.out-law.com/page-3223. Accessed 26 April 2016

PostNord (2015) E-commerce in Europe 2015. http://www.postnord.com/globalassets/global/english/document/publications/2015/en_e-commerce_in_europe_20150902.pdf. Accessed 26 April 2016

Rosner G (2014) Trustmarks in the identity ecosystem: Definitions, Use and Governance. White Paper of the Identity Steering Group. http://oixuk.org/wp-content/uploads/2014/09/Trustmarks-paper-FINAL-v2.pdf. Accessed 26 April 2016

Rule C (2002) Online Dispute Resolution for Business. Jossey-Bass, San Francisco

SafeBuy (2015) SafeBuy Code of Practice. http://care.safebuy.org.uk/code-of-practice/. Accessed 26 April 2016

Shankar V, Urban G, Sultan F (2002) Online trust: A stakeholder perspective: Concepts, implications and future directions. Journal of strategic Information systems 11:325–344. http://uploadi.www.ris.org/editor/1233300175knjiga%20online%20trust.pdf. Accessed 26 April 2016

Stanford Encyclopaedia of Philosophy (2006) Trust. http://plato.stanford.edu/entries/trust/ Accessed 26 April 2016

Der Tagesspiegel (2012) Weniger wäre besser: Allein in Deutschland gibt es fast 500 Siegel und Gütezeichen. Nun gibt es Versuche, Ordnung in das Chaos zu bringen. http://www.tagesspiegel.de/wirtschaft/weniger-waere-besser-allein-in-deutschland-gibt-es-fast-500-siegel-und-guetezeichen-nun-gibt-es-versuche-ordnung-in-das-chaos-zu-bringen/6094898.html. Accessed 26 April 2016

The Economist (2013) The rise of the sharing economy. http://www.economist.com/news/leaders/21573104-internet-everything-hire-rise-sharing-economy. Accessed 26 April 2016

The House of Lords (2016) Lords urge better protection for users of online platforms. http://www.parliament.uk/business/lords/media-centre/house-of-lords-media-notices/2016/april-2016/lords-urge-better-protection-for-users-of-online-platforms/. Accessed on 25 April 2016

TNO Innovation for Life and Intrasoft International for the European Commission DG Communications Networks, Content & Technology (2012) EU online Trustmarks: Building Digital Confidence in Europe

Trusted.ro (2014) Standarde Trusted.ro versiunea 1.2. https://www.trusted.ro/wp-content/uploads/2014/10/Standarde_Trusted_ro_oct2014.pdf. Accessed 26 April 2016

TüvSüd Group (2016) Testing and Certification Regulations. https://www.safer-shopping.de/uploads/PDF/TestingCertRegulations.pdf. Accessed 26 April 2016

TüvSüd Group (2014) Requirements catalogue for the assessment and certification of online shops, version 4.3. https://www.safer-shopping.de/uploads/PDF/Requirements_Shopsb2c.pdf. Accessed 26 April 2016

Chapter 7
The Potential for Privacy Seals in Emerging Technologies

David Barnard-Wills

Contents

Abstract This chapter examines the feasibility for privacy seals in emerging technologies focusing upon cyber-physical systems, also known as the Internet of Things (IoT). This focus provides an opportunity to compare technologies where privacy seals have purchase against those that do not, further refining the model of an effective privacy seal. It examines the privacy and data protection issues surrounding smart homes, smart cars, wearables and drones, and evaluates the potential for deploying privacy and data protection seals in these contexts by deploying design fictions. From these thought experiments, it becomes apparent that in addition to the general requirements of a privacy seal, there also needs to be

David Barnard-Wills is a Senior Research Analyst at Trilateral Research Ltd. David. barnard-wills@trilateralresearch.com. Trilateral Research Ltd. Crown House, 72 Hammersmith Road, London, W14 8TH.

D. Barnard-Wills (✉)
Trilateral Research Ltd., Crown House, 72 Hammersmith Road, London W14 8TH, UK
e-mail: David.barnard-wills@trilateralresearch.com

© T.M.C. ASSER PRESS and the authors 2018
R. Rodrigues and V. Papakonstantinou (eds.), *Privacy and Data Protection Seals*,
Information Technology and Law Series 28, https://doi.org/10.1007/978-94-6265-228-6_7

strong alignment between the technology, (including its physical design, logical design, and level of generativity) and its social context of use. By its interconnected nature, IoT fundamentally disrupts our expectations around objects (things) and information flows. Seals might act as part of the mechanisms of re-transcribing such expectations. Designing a workable seal therefore means understanding information norms, and expectations, but also desired states of information flow in particular contexts.

Keywords Internet of Things · drones · wearable computing · smart cars · privacy · security

7.1 Introduction

This chapter examines the feasibility for privacy seals in emerging technologies. Whilst privacy seals have largely been deployed in an online context, several features of this environment mitigate against their effective use. However other contexts and technologies have different affordances, dynamics of operation, and arrangements of industry stakeholders, which may provide greater opportunities for the use of privacy seals—either because a properly deployed seal may respond to privacy issues in a particular application, or because the technology inherently supports this type of certification.

This chapter will focus upon cyber-physical systems (also known as the Internet of Things—IoT), those information technologies with a physical presence as well as high levels of interconnection and the ability to collect personal data. In particular, it will examine the potential for privacy seals in relation to smart homes, smart cars, wearable technology and drones. These selected technologies are those where privacy issues and concerns have already been identified (including by EU data protection authorities and privacy and security researchers), and the use of which is currently expanding globally. This focus provides an opportunity to compare technologies where privacy seals have purchase against those that do not, further refining the model of an effective privacy seal emerging from the research literature and demonstrating *why* privacy seals have purchase.

This chapter argues that privacy protection is so variable, so context-dependent,[1] and a response to particular problems of unwanted and unwarranted information flows,[2] that a general purpose, cross-technology privacy seal is unlikely to be successful. Instead we should identify those areas where the particular dynamics of a technology-in-use in a given context, support a policy intervention through the deployment of seals, and carefully design that deployment to interface with that

---

[1] Nissenbaum 2010.

[2] Solove 2008.

context. In other cases, the many problems of privacy seals become overwhelming and the potential, desired benefits are unlikely to be achieved.

An innovative approach of this chapter is the use of design fictions—sketching out hypothetical futures of privacy seals to use them as tools to better understand the present.[3] The argument is based upon literature and conceptual analysis. The aim is therefore to explore the potential conceptual spaces for privacy seals in IoT, not to make guaranteed predictions about how they will develop. Further empirical research will be necessary, in particular the specific study and consultation of key stakeholders in the IoT industry and key regulators.

7.2   The Problems of Privacy Seals in an Online Environment

Privacy seals and data protection seals have been subject to much discussion and debate.[4] Some of this has been positive, while some of it has highlighted the limitations of privacy seals to provide privacy assurance. A problem for both data processors (often websites and other online services, such as cloud service providers) and service users, is that users essentially cannot independently determine the data protection and privacy behaviour of the processors. Privacy seals purport to solve this problem.[5] The idea of a privacy or data protection seal is that its award and display signifies that particular standards of privacy or data protection have been met. The service user can then decide if this service meets their needs, including their privacy preferences or requirements. Seals also provide a hook for privacy advocates such as non-governmental organisations (NGOs) and regulators to engage in accountability politics to ensure that organisations live up to their public commitments.[6] They are therefore aligned with other methods for increasing transparency in privacy and engaging with the complex problem of privacy online (such as simple/readable privacy policies, machine-readable privacy preferences, and transparency activism).[7]

The European Commission funded EU Privacy Seals study[8] examined existing privacy and data protection seal schemes, and related information security seals and seal-based certification schemes in other policy areas (including telecommunications, banking and finance and environmental regulation). From this comparative analysis, the researchers were able to determine a set of criteria for the design and

---

[3] Dunne and Raby 2013, p. 3.

[4] Rodrigues et al. 2013a, 2016; Stanaland et al. 2011; Connolly 2008; LaRose and Rifon 2006; Moores 2005; Moores and Dhillon 2003; Cline 2003.

[5] Rodrigues et al. 2016.

[6] Bennett 2008, p. 14.

[7] Barnard-Wills and Ashenden 2015, p. 144.

[8] Rodrigues et al. 2013b.

operation of an effective privacy seal scheme. Some of these apply across any well-managed certification scheme: e.g., clear objectives and scope, harmonised rules across countries, robust certification criteria, a sound basis for standards, cooperation between involved standards bodies in a field (avoiding contradictory requirements) and regular review of the scheme.[9] In the hypothetical design fictions that follow, these potential schemes are assumed to have met (or exceeded) these base-line functional requirements. This is not an easy task, but these are essential pre-requisites for effective operation of any privacy seal.

Unfortunately, the current context of privacy and data protection seals falls short of achieving the potential benefits desired of them. Both Rodrigues et al.,[10] and Balboni[11] in this volume present an overview of the controversies, concerns and challenges relating to existing privacy and data protection seal schemes. In general, poor organisation, limited transparency, poor quality of verification and lack of clarity about what is being certified. The EU Privacy Seals study,[12] found that many existing schemes do not propose specific guarantees about the protection of personal data, and those schemes that are more specifically focussed on data protection (aligned with EU law) have reached a limited audience so far. Many of the schemes (being based outside the EU although available and visible within) do not cover international transfers of personal data.[13] The privacy and data protection elements of existing schemes are variable and inconsistent. The regulatory and compliance standards underlying these schemes are a patchwork of legal criteria derived from data protection law and industry created criteria. Privacy and data protection seals are, therefore, a heterogeneous field with recurrent issues surrounding their coverage, claims and validity, but at the same time bringing benefits to various stakeholders such as users of a seal and consumers. In short, they provide limited benefits to individuals and many entities that could be certified tend to avoid them, thus in turn reducing their benefits to policy makers and to the economy.

A report by the French data protection authority Commission Nationale de L'informatique et des Libertés (CNIL) stated that:

> The difficulty also lies in knowing what one is labelling: is it a company, a specific data processing process or a product? It is not just isolated technological elements that must be labelled, but rather everything that depends on data. It has to take account of the whole information collection and processing process and subsequent onward sale. A system that combined a standard of this type and awareness raising among consumers regarding their personal data could encourage companies to certify their transparency and their excellence in the field of data processing.[14]

---

[9] Rodrigues et al. 2014.

[10] Rodrigues et al. 2016.

[11] Chapter 6 of this volume.

[12] Rodrigues et al. 2013b, 2014.

[13] Particularly relevant given ongoing discussions around the failure of the Safe Harbour transfer agreement between the US and the EU.

[14] CNIL 2012, p. 50.

Privacy seals are also problematic in the malleable, but black-box world that Pasquale describes—users are poorly positioned to know what companies do with their data due to secrecy, legal secrecy and obfuscation.[15] Privacy seals are also implicated in the fundamental asymmetry between the parties who award, make use of, or make decisions upon the basis of the seal. In the information security context, this has been referred to as the "Market for Silver Bullets", and many of the same problems, such as the lack of approachable metrics of quality, apply to privacy products and claims, including seals. Grigg describes the problem as follows:

> Security goods, when they exhibit poor testability and the presence or perception of active and aggressive third party attackers, place themselves in a very difficult space. By lack of approachable metrics of quality, buyers lack sufficient information to support a purchasing decision. Likewise, sellers are stymied by the attacker's refusal to hold to theoretical and statistical models. It is likely that at least in some security markets the seller also lacks sufficient information. Asymmetric prescriptions of information sharing will be inadequate as there is none to share, and will likely raise institutional, signalling and screening costs that make matters worse.[16]

7.3   The Argument for Focused and Specific Privacy Seals

Several of the core issues of privacy seals arise from an attempt to produce a general-purpose claim about privacy practices. Claims which can be used in multiple, quite distinct contexts and which do not default back to simply being claims about processing in compliance with some set of relatively abstract standards, may not map particularly well to the privacy dynamics of a given situation. In the EU, the key factor in this context will most likely be data protection law (currently Directive 95/46/EC, but being replaced by the General Data Protection Regulation (GDPR)),[17] but other sets of standards such as the OECD[18] Privacy Principles[19] or the US Fair Information Practice Principles (FIPP)[20] are also possible.

Most privacy seals in use address the privacy and data protection behaviour of websites. It is arguable that many of the problems of privacy seals emerge from the openness and malleability of digital environments, and from the fast-moving culture of online technology, dominated by advertising revenue, where disruption and finding new uses for collected data are lauded and seen as good vehicles for investment capital.[21] This is what Jonathan Zittrain terms "generativity": a system's

---

[15] Pasquale 2015.

[16] Grigg 2008.

[17] European Parliament and Council 2016.

[18] Organisation for Economic Co-operation and Development.

[19] OECD 2013.

[20] Federal Trade Commission 2007.

[21] Morozov 2013.

capacity to produce unanticipated change through unfiltered contributions from broad and varied audiences.[22] Zittrain uses the term to differentiate between information technology that can easily be repurposed by the user, without the permission of the creator (and thereby used in original, unanticipated and creative ways), and walled gardens where only approved uses are possible (for example, the Apple App Store). For Zittrain, the term is largely positive, associated with innovation and democratic power, however, generativity intersects with privacy in several ways. Firstly, a feature of information technology is that it can be very rapidly be adapted. For privacy purposes, it can be very important how a piece of data is treated, processed or stored, but in a generative device, this can change very rapidly. As an example, imagine an app such as SnapChat, which promised short-lived messages that would not be saved. A second app can be created, which allows a user to capture screenshots of the supposedly ephemeral message, changing the privacy claims that can be made about it. In relation to privacy seals, generativity fundamentally means that any labelling on the technology, or in effect any statement about how the technology is processing information, can be rendered incorrect, rapidly and without apparent visual change.

Given this problem, it may be more appropriate to investigate the possibilities of privacy seals designed for narrower user-cases than "online", perhaps for specific technologies or specific industries. There are examples of very specific seals already established in areas of information technology. For example, the EuroRec EHR Quality Seal for Electronic Health Record systems,[23] TRUSTe's Smart Grid Privacy Certification,[24] and the Market Research Society's (MRS) Fair Data certification.[25] There is also theoretical support for this narrowing of focus. There is a school of thought that posits that privacy violations are experienced based upon contextual expectations about the flow of information—when information does not flow in accordance with the social norms of a given socio-cultural context.[26] In this case, contextually defined privacy seals may be able to make more meaningful statements about information flows. The level of abstraction shifts from "Data collected on you is secured and used in an appropriate way" to (for example) "the data collected from the sensors in the car is encrypted, and transmitted only to servers controlled by the manufacturer". Similarly, the principles the adherence to which are being certified can be more specific and more closely related to a given industry or context. The EuroRec seal makes claims about how a system meets a particular set of requirements for health records, whilst the MRS certification states that a website collecting data for the purposes of market research will treat collected data in line with a set of industry-generated commitments. Third, given the

---

[22] Zittrain 2006.

[23] See http://www.eurorec.org/services/seal/index.cfm. Accessed 9 March 2016.

[24] TRUSTe, "TRUSTed Smart Grid Privacy Certification". https://www.truste.com/business-products/trusted-smart-grid/. Accessed 9 March 2016.

[25] See http://www.fairdata.org.uk/. Accessed 9 March 2016.

[26] Nissenbaum 2010.

grounding in a specific context, the claims made are actually contextualised, and may be easier for relying parties (consumers in many contexts) to understand (although this would be open to empirical challenge). The EU Privacy Seals study also found there were variable cases to be made for privacy seals in a range of areas (the study examined CCTV systems, international transfers of data in cloud computing, smart electricity meters and biometric systems).[27] The real differences in the way that the technologies were purchased, used, administered and regulated that changed the context for the use of privacy seals in ways which would be likely to affect the utility of those seals for (also divergent) policy goals in those particular areas.

7.4 The Potential for Privacy Seals in Cyber-Physical Technologies

For the purposes of this chapter we will pick as our working focus various elements of the Internet of Things (IoT), context aware electronic systems that interact with their physical surroundings.[28] Other possibilities for focused seals might include big data, messaging software, genetic analytics services, facial recognition, social media and numerous other sites of specific impact. IoT is a suitable topic because it is currently growing in use and as an emergent technology in the early stages of its privacy problems, early intervention may be particularly effective, whilst at the same time having a high degree of contextual variation within its envisaged deployment. Another relevant element of IoT systems is that they, to a limited extent, have different levels of generativity. The physical component of such systems can put some limits on this generativity of the technology. For example, a smart home sensor is likely located in a specific place, the majority of a small drone's carrying capacity is taken up with the systems necessary to achieve flight, communication and delivery of the appropriate payload. IoT is also useful as its physical objects (it's "Things") do sit unquestionably within specific legal jurisdictions, meaning that certification can be tied to legislation more directly.

IoT (such as smart cities, cars, homes etc.) involves the proliferation of low-cost sensors and actuators throughout the environment, and the interconnection of these devices with each other and with the online environment.[29] The aim of such systems is to increase efficiency and control, but they also create potential privacy (and security) risks, depending upon the way the technologies are set up and used. The increased number of sensors and activity logs provide a source of close, granular and intimate personal data on the activities and behaviour of inhabitants and visitors. The IoT is therefore a point of intense contact between networked information

---

[27] De Hert et al. 2014.

[28] Das et al. 2012; Banerjee et al. 2012.

[29] IEEE 2015.

technology and physical space.[30] Trends in IoT suggest that developers wish to pursue the "digital mesh" where more and more devices are interconnected, increased machine learning and "ambient user experience" where interaction with IoT devices and services becomes more seamless across devices, and less formal and screen based.[31]

The approach adopted here is to consider thought experiments around specific IoT technologies (i.e., smart homes, smart cars, wearable technology and drones),[32] the privacy risks they pose, and which features of these systems and their social context might support or undermine the use of privacy seals, and to reflect upon what might be meaningfully signified by a seal in these contexts. In general, IoT raises issues related to integration of different data sources, data leakage at various points in the "mesh", data ownership, consent,[33] and ubiquitous surveillance. The Article 29 Data Protection Working Party's Opinion on IoT identifies it as a key area for privacy and gives a strong opening for seals as part of a consent system, stating that:

> Users must remain in complete control of their personal data throughout the product lifecycle and when organisations rely on consent as a basis for processing, the consent should be fully informed, freely given and specific.[34]

7.4.1 Smart Homes

Smart homes are houses (and other buildings) equipped with technology that provides the occupants with comprehensive information about the state of the home and allow them to control all connected devices, including remotely.[35] The increased number of interlinked sensors and activity logs present and active in the smart home will be a source of close, granular and intimate data on the activities and behaviour of inhabitants and visitors. The home is a key site of consumption, and given the intimate, non-public context, behaviour in the home might be viewed as more meaningful or authentic than public activity. This means that the data produced by such environments will have commercial (e.g., insurance, advertising, financial) and law enforcement value, and there will be resulting privacy and data protection debates arising from this. The risks that arise from smart home privacy are probabilistic rather than deterministic, and can therefore be hard to communicate. Function creep is highly likely in the smart home context. Much of the smart home literature,

---

[30] IEEE 2015, p. iv.

[31] Levy 2015.

[32] Dunne and Raby 2013.

[33] Edwards 2016.

[34] Article 29 Data Protection Working Party 2014.

[35] Barnard-Wills et al. 2014.

and particularly the promotional and marketing literature for smart devices, starts from the assumption that the occupant of the smart home is the owner. In many cases, such as rented accommodation and commercial building automation, this will not be the case. In these contexts, smart homes provide for surveillance, and for automatic enforcement of policies set by the owner. Smart homes also provide the capacity for potentially intense surveillance of other family members.[36]

Aspects of smart homes that support the deployment of privacy seals include accepted ownership models for home appliances that are not advertising revenue driven. Users may be able to make informed choices between different smart devices based upon privacy-relevant features that could be easily symbolised (for example, an icon to demonstrate if a device uses cloud or local storage for any data it collects). Smart home devices are often of a physical size that can support a visible seal and customers are relatively accustomed to looking for these (many electrical items will already be carrying the CE mark for example). Compatibility and interconnection across devices are key issues for smart homes and if privacy controls could potentially be integrated with the emergent interoperability standards. Further entire product ranges (and the way they network together) could be certified as opposed to individual items.

Design Fiction: The Rental Privacy Seal

In the near future, this hypothetical seal has become a necessity for rental properties, much like a gas-fitter's certificate. It provides renters of smart homes with reassurance that data collected about them is not being misused by their landlord (that any data collected by the smart home complies with privacy standards). The landlord pledges to reduce and limit the data collected to only that necessary for the provision of agreed services, and the integrity and safety of the property. Landlords will ensure that any data transmitted is made visible to the inhabitants and information is provided in advance of any changes in means of collection, transmission or sharing.

7.4.2   Smart Cars

The transport industry is increasingly a heavy collector and processor of data (including personal information). Modern cars include high numbers of sensors and microprocessors, and have even been termed "a computer that you put your body inside".[37] These sensors are increasingly communicating within the car but also externally. This development started with security systems that could report the location of a stolen car (and potential disable key systems remotely) and satellite navigation, and has been picked up by insurance companies offering discounted insurance products to car

---

[36] Barnard-Wills et al. 2014, p. 55.

[37] Doctorow 2012.

owners willing to fit a black-box that provides the insurance company with telemetry data on driving behaviour. This trend is pointing towards fully-automated self-driving cars is being developed by Google and others in the automotive industry. For example, the Mercedes F105 concept car envisages the interior as a "digital living space" able to respond to gestures and input to multiple touchscreens.[38]

Self-driving cars are extremely heavy data collectors and processors. They make use of machine learning and collect significant information on their surroundings in order to deal with the complex computational problem of navigating a heavy, fast vehicle through space without collision or injury. The cars are also highly connected, and there are high potential benefits from sharing data between cars, and between cars and their environment. For example, cars might coordinate to reduce the space between them allowing more cars to a given area of road at a particular speed. The cars are likely to transmit significant information or a personal and granular nature to either the manufacturer or the owner (in the case of rental or on-demand car services). For example, it would be easy from this data to identify the likely home of a car user. Hacking threats and vulnerabilities in smart cars have already been identified.[39] In addition, the recent scandal surrounding revelations that Volkswagen had engineered the software in some of its cars to reduce engine emissions under test conditions whilst having higher emissions (and presumably greater performance) under real-world driving conditions, suggests that there are elements lacking in the current automotive testing regimes.

Several elements of the nature of smart cars (including self-driving cars) support the development and use of privacy standards and certification, including privacy seals.

First, the automotive industry is (in comparison to the online world) centred around a relatively small number of major players. These key players are used to managing their complex supply chains from smaller component manufacturers, and are able to exercise significant influence over this ecosystem. Therefore, if the top-level players were willing to mandate certain features from their suppliers, then they are likely to be able to achieve this. This provides support to establishing infrastructure that will support some elements of privacy-preserving behaviour (for example strong device identification, encrypted communications between smart components, etc.). It does require the key players to be willing to demand these features, and does not ensure that privacy-protecting smart cars are actually built out of these components, but this level of hierarchy in a market place does support the spread of standards. Privacy certification could be made a pre-requisite for access to smart car data for other parts of the supply chain, where it could be valuable for improving performance and quality. It also provides a tool for

---

[38] Mercedes Benz 2016.
[39] Rouf et al. 2010.

manufacturers to better understand how sub-systems in a complex smart car will interact.[40]

Second, cars remain a high value-purchase, one of the most significant (other than a home) that many consumers will make. This is a significant difference from the environment of online privacy seals, which are often related to free services supported by advertising revenue. Whilst there may be incentives for car manufacturers to make better use of the data generated by smart cars, there are also potentially competing incentives to provide customers with a particular privacy position or attitude towards data handling, in a way that does not conflict with their core business proposition (advertising and privacy protection may sometimes be seen to be in fundamental conflict). Whilst all connected devices increase privacy risks over their less smart predecessors, Forrest makes the argument that cars are more embedded into societies than smart lightbulbs, which only attract minority interest.[41]

Third, car manufacturers look for features that differentiate their vehicles from their competitors. At the luxury end of the automotive market this increasingly includes technological features (including some of the smart functionality such as assisted parking, lane following technologies and assisted hazard avoidance). As technologies mature, some of these features filter down over time to more price-conscious sections of the market. Privacy and information security could well serve as such differentiators, particularly for those automotive brands that have made physical safety and reliability a core part of their brand identity. The industry has also demonstrated some attention to the role that privacy and IT security play: in his presentation on vehicle connectivity at the Fully Networked Car 2013 conference, Dr. Matthias Klauda of Bosch Automotive Systems Integration Corporate Department highlighted the IT security issue and aspects to tackle to protect the integrity and functionality of vehicle systems and the privacy of users.[42]

Finally, the automotive industry has long experience with standards and certification, with many elements of cars, their manufacture and their testing being assessed against, and certified to particular standards e.g., ISO/TS16949 on supply chain quality management or ISO-26262 family of standards on Road Vehicles Functional Safety. This gives the industry significant familiarity with the standardisation and certification processes which can be applied to meeting requirements around privacy and data protection in relation to smart cars. Smart cars are themselves an area of current standards development. For example, the International Standards Organization (ISO) is currently developing standard ISO 15638 Telematics Applications for Regulated commercial vehicles (TARV). This is based around the communications technologies for communication between cars and infrastructure, and reflects over a decade's development work in the area.[43]

---

[40] Forrest 2016.

[41] Forrest 2016.

[42] Tranchard 2013.

[43] Gasiorowski-Denis 2014.

Additionally, the industry has also proved able to respond to government regulation driving the adoption of particular standards, for example, Regulation (EC) 443/2009 on emission performance standards[44] (even if there are some rule-breakers).

Design Fiction—The Smart Car Privacy Seal

A consortium of European automobile manufacturers adopted the Vehicle Communication Privacy standard in 2019 based upon a model first developed by BMW's luxury vehicle division. Initially deployed in partnership with Uber and Lyft, the standard guaranteed privacy for passengers of personal limo services targeted at business executives, who need communication and connectivity on the move but require commercial confidentiality. After gaining considerable support from politicians, the standard has since proliferated through to the more general car market as an optional upgrade. It covers the data shared between smart components in the car, as well as that transmitted outside of the car. It also includes protocols for the deletion of user data when a car is sold or transferred to a new owner.

7.4.3   Wearable Technologies

"Wearables" encompass internet connected technology that can be worn on the body. The most common are activity/fitness trackers and smart watches.[45] Google Glass style augmented reality headsets also fit into this category. The privacy implications of wearables arise because they often collect sensitive health-related data, in real time, which can often reveal unexpected information about an individual, whilst are often designed to be used passively and forgotten about through the day and to integrate seamlessly into your life.[46] They can also conduct "sousveillance" of the wearer's surroundings.[47] Additionally, many wearables are produced by small companies (including start-ups) with the potential for bankruptcy risks, data aggregation, data "land-grabs", and they can be difficult to patch and update.[48]

Because of the small form factor of wearable devices, traditional consent models of "notice and choice" are problematic (exacerbating the problem found with small mobile screens). This might provide an avenue for privacy seals, and seals to potentially support the "flexible" approach to regulation that the Future for Privacy Forum sees as necessary in the nascent wearables market.[49] An interesting development is the potential for machine-readable seals deployed in the physical world

---

[44] European Parliament and the Council 2009.

[45] Wolf et al. 2015.

[46] Alton 2015.

[47] Genaro Motti and Caine 2015.

[48] Maddox 2015.

[49] Wolf et al. 2015.

that can signal to augmented reality devices that particular privacy behaviours are to be followed (for example, imagine a seal that instructs Google Glass to stop recording, much like the "ugliest shirt in the word" in William Gibson's novel *Zero History*).[50] However, the "forgettability" of commercial wearables is antithetical to the use of seals. This is because their designers want the device to collect "authentic" data, with fewer gaps, and this requires the user to become accustomed to the presence of the device, and not to think too much about the data flowing through it.[51] In many ways, wearables are constructed not to trigger panoptic effects. This suggests that seals and certification in wearables will not occur in the consumer market, but may be more likely in regulated and professionalised fields. There is evidence of interest in security and privacy certification in relation to wearables.[52]

Design Fiction: Secure Hospitals Mark—The Wearable Technology Seal

Privacy seals found little purchase in consumer wearables such as augmented reality glasses or fitness and activity trackers. However, when similar technologies were deployed in the more heavily regulated world of medicine and healthcare, both patients and healthcare providers sought out more verified guarantees about how such devices shared sensitive health-related information. Hospitals found value in providing outpatients with wearables to monitor recovery; however, they needed to be able to guarantee that this data was securely transmitted and stored. The seal on the medical wearable demonstrates that the device meets high quality standards for encryption. A parallel seal was developed for smart hospitals to demonstrate that their systems were capable of secure interoperability with the secure wearables, and that only medical professionals involved in the specific care of individual patients could access data from their wearables.

7.4.4   Drones

Drones (also known as unmanned aerial vehicles (UAV) or Remotely Piloted Aircraft Systems (RPAS) are a varied and emerging technology with clear impacts for privacy and also for data protection, in particular in their use for law enforcement purposes, but also in civilian applications. A report produced by the European RPAS Steering Group suggested a key capability of drones was their ability to perform tasks that manned systems cannot, either for safety or economic reasons.[53] Several features of drones contribute towards their impact on privacy: drones provide new platforms and angles for visual surveillance, can avoid ground-level barriers and congestion, and can combine with other surveillance

---

[50] Krombholz et al. 2015.
[51] Alton 2015.
[52] Hamblen 2015.
[53] European RPAS Steering Group 2013, p. 5.

infrastructures.[54] Drones can place larger areas under surveillance and for greater periods.[55] Compared with closed-circuit television (CCTV), drones can be equipped with various payloads, can process different types of information, are not fixed to a single place, can enter private spaces, and can be deployed rapidly. They can also observe and follow individuals, increasing the breadth and duration of surveillance. These capabilities can have a significant impact upon privacy of individuals, particularly in public and semi-public places.

A report on the privacy and data protection implications of drones, produced for the European Commission (EC) found several features of drones bring their operation into conflict with EU data protection legislation.[56] Because many drones are small, nearly silent and therefore practically invisible at altitude, it can be difficult to meet transparency, accountability and consent obligations.[57] Additionally, it can be very unclear what data is being transmitted from the drone to the operator, and for what purposes this is being processed. This lack of visibility (a "double invisibility")[58] also increases the possibility of a panoptic or chilling effect[59] whilst at the same time increasing the risk of voyeurism and distancing the observer from the observed. A photograph of a person is personal data and with appropriate sensors drones can collect images and many other types of personal data. Being aerial, drones are likely to incidentally collect personal data, thus infringe data protection rights. The EC report found that privacy concerns not only related to drones as an aircraft, but also to the payload or software with which the drone is fitted.[60] However, this report found that drones did not present *new* data protection issues (their payloads are not new) and that the operation of drones (from a data protection and privacy perspective), could be regulated through either existing data protection legislation, or under the new framework of the GDPR. An American Civil Liberties Union (ACLU) study added concerns around discriminatory targeting, institutional abuse, and automated enforcement, identifying drones as part of a trend towards law enforcement without human decision makers.[61]

The Article 29 Data Protection Working Party's Opinion on drones reiterates many of these points, and found that "the relevant point from a privacy and data protection standpoint is not the drone per se but the data processing equipment on board the drone and the subsequent processing of personal data that may take place,"[62] and that the "potential impact of the privacy intrusion is compounded by

---

[54] Clarke 2014a, pp. 230–246.
[55] Clarke 2014b, pp. 247–262.
[56] Finn et al. 2014.
[57] Ibid., p. 14.
[58] Fossool 2008, pp. 149–50.
[59] Finn et al. 2014.
[60] Finn et al. 2014.
[61] Stanley and Crump 2011, p. 12.
[62] Article 29 Data Protection Working Party 2015, p. 7.

the wide constellation of stakeholders and entities involved in their use".[63] The Opinion highlights the issue of data ownership, and the requirement for clear identification of controller and processor, and further, the potential for the use of drones to fundamentally transform the activities of law enforcement and in particular the role of data in guiding law enforcement actions.[64] Finally, the report advocates the use of data protection impact assessments in the deployment and use of drones. Future technological advances are expected to increase the range and duration of drone operation, whilst at the same time reducing size and cost, thereby increasing stealth and surveillance capacities.[65] An European Data Protection Supervisor (EDPS) Opinion on drones in civil aviation underlines the importance of privacy enhancing technologies (PETs) to ensure efficacy against privacy breaches (it includes Privacy-by-design and privacy-by-default principles and privacy impact assessments for the use of drones).[66,67]

Drones will often be deployed by organisations for particular purposes—focused privacy seals may have greater purchase in business-to-business decisions. Complex cyber-physical systems are often combined from other smaller components, modules and sub-systems. If the developers of the end-product or service wish to make particular commitments around privacy to their eventual customers, they themselves may be in the market for sub-systems which meet particular standards. Business are arguably often better placed to verify that commitments have been met than end-users. The primary disadvantage of drones for the use of privacy seals is related to the "double invisibility" mentioned previously. Smaller drones, or drones operating at a distinct distance are hard to perceive, meaning that any markings on the exterior of the drone are likely imperceptible to any potential data subjects. Seals would therefore have to be an addition to any signage that might be deployed to inform people that a drone was being operated, by whom and for what purpose (as is increasingly suggested/required by guidance on the commercial use of drones published by EU data protection authorities.[68] The Article 29 Working party's Opinion suggested:

> The promotion of Codes of conduct and/or certification schemes for manufacturers and operators could be envisaged in order to improve civil drone operators' awareness and understanding of data protection issues as well as with a view to help DPAs monitor compliance. .... Finally, a helpful role could be played also by privacy seals. Even though such schemes shall not excuse data controllers from knowledge of their data protection and privacy commitments, the participation of drone operators and manufacturers in a general

---

[63] Article 29 Data Protection Working Party 2015, p. 8.

[64] Article 29 Data Protection Working Party 2015, p. 10.

[65] Stanley and Crump 2011, December 2011.

[66] European Data Protection Supervisor 2014.

[67] Pauner and Viguri 2015.

[68] See for example https://ico.org.uk/for-the-public/drones and http://www.dataprotection.ie/docs/guidance-on-the-use-of-drone-aircraft/1510.htm. Accessed 3 March 2017.

privacy seal approach could be supported as a means towards accountability and compliance.[69]

Design Fiction—The Drone Operator's Privacy and Data Protection Certificate

Building upon the Basic National UAS Certificate (BNUC^tm) introduced by the now-defunct EuroUSC in 2007, and subsequently picked up by other training providers,[70] then developed in cooperation with data protection authorities of EU Member States, the seal certifies that the drone operator has undergone training on the relevant data protection and privacy concerns of drone operation, compliant with the GDPR, including how to perform an appropriate privacy and data protection impact assessment focusing upon identifying appropriate grounds for data processing, the need for prior authorisation, purpose limitation, informing the public, and protection and anonymisation of collected personal data. It has proved popular with contractors, who can demonstrate to clients that they are familiar with data protection issues surrounding drones and are less likely to create data protection concerns for the client (who as the data controller remains responsible).

7.5   Conclusion

What then is the potential of privacy and data protection seals for IoT, and what does this tell us about emerging technologies and privacy seals themselves? From these thought experiments, it becomes apparent that in addition to the general requirements of a privacy seal, we also need strong alignment between the technology, including its physical design, logical design, and level of generativity, and its social context of use, including ownership, how people get and process information, location within the politics of infrastructure,[71] and other very complex social relations.

For a seal to "work", it must be integrated with, for example, car user patterns or home ownership models. These are very subtle (a rental car differs from a truck, from a sports car) and implies a requirement for a deep "industrial sociology". It is impossible to certify "all good things" but more feasible to assert certain specific patterns of digital and organisation behaviour. Aaron Straup Cope has written, "In 2016 the cognitive overhead of not simply understanding what an object does but what an object *might* do, particularly when it is connected to the internet is overwhelming, on good days. On bad days, it can feel like a betrayal".[72] By its (interconnected) nature, IoT fundamentally disrupts our expectations around objects

---

[69] Article 29 Data Protection Working Party 2015, p. 18.

[70] http://www.flyby-technology.com/blog/eurousc-and-bnuc-s-graduates?gclid=CNGl1tqTutICFW i17Qod5_kKFA Accessed 3 March 2017.

[71] Easterling 2014.

[72] Cope 2016.

(things) and information flows. Seals might act as part of the mechanisms of re-transcribing such expectations. Designing a workable seal therefore means understanding information norms, and expectations, but also desired states of information flow in particular contexts. This requires multi-disciplinary research from industrial knowledge, social science, technology-focused ethnography, and context-focused ethnography, with attention to specific privacy concerns. This will then provide the "grip" necessary for privacy seals when a seal can make a strong link between a socially or psychologically desired state and the particular technology and context, and the mechanics, criteria and claims of the privacy seal.

References

Alton L (2015) How wearable tech could spark a new privacy revolution. Techcrunch http://techcrunch.com/2015/09/12/how-wearable-tech-could-spark-a-new-privacy-revolution/. Accessed 1 July 2016

Article 29 Data Protection Working Party (2014) Opinion 8/2014 on Recent Developments on the Internet of Things. WP223, Brussels

Article 29 Data Protection Working Party (2015) Opinion 01/2015 on Privacy and Data Protection Issues relating to the utilisation of drones, Brussels. http://ec.europa.eu/justice/data-protection/article-29/documentation/opinion-recommendation/files/2015/wp231_en.pdf. Accessed 1 July 2016

Banerjee A, Venkatasubramanian K, Mukherjee T, Gupta S (2012) Ensuring safety, security, and sustainability of mission-critical cyber physical systems. Proceedings of the IEEE, vol. 100: 283–299

Barnard-Wills D, Ashenden D (2015) Playing with Privacy: Games for education and communication in the politics of online privacy. Political Studies 63:142–160

Barnard-Wills D, Marino L, Portesi S (2014) Threat Landscape and good practice guide for smart homes and converged media. ENISA, Heraklion

Bennett C (2008) The privacy advocates: Resisting the spread of surveillance. MIT Press, Cambridge, MA/London

Clarke R (2014a) Understanding the drone epidemic. Computer law & security review 30

Clarke R (2014b) What drones inherit from their ancestors. Computer law & security review 30

Cline J (2003) Web site privacy seals: Are they worth it? Computerworld. http://www.computerworld.com/article/2569776/e-commerce/web-site-privacy-seals--are-they-worth-it-.html. Accessed 1 July 2016

CNIL (2012) Privacy Towards 2020: Expert Views, IP Reports, Innovation & Foresight, no. 01. https://www.cnil.fr/sites/default/files/typo/document/CAHIER_IP_EN2.pdf. Accessed 1 July 2016

Connolly C (2008) Trust Mark Schemes Struggle to Protect Privacy 2008. Galexia, Version 1.0, 26 Sept 2008. http://www.galexia.com/public/research/assets/trustmarks_struggle_20080926. Accessed 1 July 2016

Cope A (2016) The Pendulum of Bespokiness. Aaronland. http://www.aaronland.info/weblog/2016/03/09/osha/. Accessed 1 July 2016.

Das SK, Kant K, Zhang N (2012) Handbook on securing cyberphysical critical infrastructure. Morgan Kaufmann, Burlington, MA

De Hert P, Papakonstantinou V, Rodrigues R, Barnard-Wills D, Wright D, Remotti L, Damvekerakaki T (2014) Challenges and possible scope of an EU privacy seal scheme. Second Interim technical report, Study on EU privacy seals

Doctorow C (2012) What's inside the box. Locus Online. http://www.locusmag.com/Perspectives/2012/03/cory-doctorow-whats-inside-the-box/. Accessed 1 July 2016

Dunne A, Raby F (2013) Speculative Everything: Design, Fiction and Social Dreaming. MIT Press, Cambridge, MA

Easterling K (2014) Extrastatecraft: The power of infrastructure space. Verso, London

Edwards L (2016) Privacy, Security and Data Protection in Smart Cities: A Critical EU Law Perspective. European Data Protection Law Review, forthcoming. Available at SSRN: http://ssrn.com/abstract=2711290. Accessed 1 July 2016

European Data Protection Supervisor (2014) Opinion on the Communication from the Commission to the European Parliament and the Council on "A new era for aviation - opening the aviation market to the civil use of remotely piloted aircraft systems in a safe and sustainable manner". Brussels

European Parliament and the Council, Regulation (EC) No 443/2009 of the European Parliament and the Council of 23 April 2009 Setting emission performance standards for new passenger cars as part of the Community's integrated approach to reduce CO2 emissions from light duty vehicles, OJ L 140 5.6.2009, pp. 1–15

European Parliament and the Council, Regulation (EU) 2016/679 of the European Parliament and the Council of 27 April 2016 on the protection of natural persons with regard to the processing of personal data and on the free movement of such data, and repealing Directives 95/46/EC (General Data Protection Regulation), OJ L 119 4.5.2016., pp. 1–88. http://eur-lex.europa.eu/legal-content/EN/TXT/?uri=CELEX:32016R0679

European RPAS Steering Group (2013) Roadmap for the integration of civil remotely piloted aircraft systems to the European Aviation System

Federal Trade Commission (2007) Fair Information Practice Principles. Archived 31 March 2009 at the Wayback Machine: https://web.archive.org/web/20090331134113/http://www.ftc.gov/reports/privacy3/fairinfo.shtm. Accessed 11 May 2017

Finn RL, Wright D, Donavan A, Jacques L, De Hert P (2014) Privacy, Data Protection and Ethical Risks in Civil RPAS Operations, D3.3. Final Report for the European Commission, 7 November 2014. http://ec.europa.eu/DocsRoom/documents/8550. Accessed 3 March 2017

Forrest C (2016) Why the connected car is one of this generation's biggest security risks. Zdenet.com. www.zdnet.com/article/why-the-connected-car-is-one-of-this-generations-biggest-security-risks/. Accessed 1 July 2016

Fossool V (2008) RFID et biométrie - état delieuex. In: Docquin B, Pullemans A (eds) Actualities du droit de la vie privée. Bruylant, Brussels, pp. 149–50

Gasiorowski-Denis E (2014) ISO Suite of standards kicks the connected car into gear. ISO News. http://www.iso.org/iso/home/news_index/news_archive/news.htm?Refid=Ref1896. Accessed 1 July 2016

Genaro Motti E, Caine K (2015) Users' privacy concerns about wearables: Impact and form factor, sensors and type of data collected. Fa15 IFCC Proceeding

Grigg I (2008) The Market for Silver Bullets. http://iang.org/papers/market_for_silver_bullets.html. Accessed 9 March 2016

Hamblen C (2015) UL creating standard for wearable privacy and security. Computerworld. http://www.computerworld.com/article/2991331/security/ul-creating-standard-for-wearable-privacy-and-security.html. Accessed 1 July 2016

IEEE (2015) Towards a definition of the Internet of Things (IoT). 1. IEEE Internet Initiative. http://iot.ieee.org/images/files/pdf/IEEE_IoT_Towards_Definition_Internet_of_Things_Issue1_14MAY15.pdf. Accessed 1 July 2016

Krombholz K, Dabrowski A, Smith M, Weippl E (2015) OK Glass, Leave me Alone: Towards a Systematization of Privacy Enhancing Technologies for Wearable Computing. 1st Workshop on Wearable Security and Privacy, Financial Crypto 2015, Puerto Rico, 30.01.2015. In: Financial Cryptography and Data Security FC 2015 International Workshops, Springer

LaRose R, Rifon N (2006) Your privacy is assured – of being disturbed: Websites with and without privacy seals. New Media & Society 8, pp. 1009–1029

Levy H (2015) Top 10 technology trends signal the digital mesh. Gartner. https://www.gartner.com/smarterwithgartner/top-ten-technology-trends-signal-the-digital-mesh/. Accessed 1 July 2016

Maddox T (2015) The dark side of wearables: How they're secretly jeopardising your security and privacy. Tech Republic. http://www.techrepublic.com/article/the-dark-side-of-wearables-how-theyre-secretly-jeopardizing-your-security-and-privacy/. Accessed 9 March 2016

Mercedes Benz (2016) https://www.mercedes-benz.com/en/mercedes-benz/innovation/research-vehicle-f-015-luxury-in-motion/. Accessed 1 July 2016

Moores T (2005) Do consumers understand the role of privacy seals in e-commerce? Communications of the ACM. 48: 86–91

Moores T, Dhillon G (2003) Do privacy seals in e-commerce really work? Communications of the ACM - Mobile computing opportunities and challenges. 46:265–271

Morozov E (2013) To Save Everything, Click Here: Technology, Solutionism and the Urge to Fix Problems That Don't Exist. Penguin, UK

Nissenbaum H (2010) Privacy in Context: Technology, Policy and the Integrity of Social Life. Stanford Law Books, Stanford, CA

OECD (2013) Guidelines on the Protection of Privacy and Transborder Flows of Personal Data. http://www.oecd.org/sti/ieconomy/oecdguidelinesontheprotectionofprivacyandtransborderflows-ofpersonaldata.htm. Accessed 09 March 2016

Pasquale F (2015) The Black Box Society: The Secret Algorithms That Control Money and Information. Harvard University Press, Cambridge, MA

Pauner C, Viguri J (2015) A legal approach to civilian use of drones. Privacy and personal data protection concerns. Democracy and Security Review 5. http://www.democraziaesicurezza.it/Saggi/A-Legal-Approach-to-Civilian-Use-of-Drones-in-Europe.-Privacy-and-Personal-Data-Protection-Concerns

Rodrigues R, Barnard-Wills D, De Hert P, Papakonstantinou V (2016) The future of a European Data Protection Seal: An exploration of policy options under the new data protection regime. International Review of Law, Computers and Technology

Rodrigues R, Barnard-Wills D, Wright D, Beslay L, Dubois N, De Hert P, Papakonstantinou V (2013) EU Privacy Seals Project: Inventory and Analysius of Privacy Certification Schemes. European Commission. http://bookshop.europa.eu/en/eu-privacy-seals-project-pbLBNA26190/?CatalogCategoryID=CXoKABst5TsAAAEjepEY4e5L2013. Accessed 1 July 2016

Rodrigues R, Barnard-Wills D, Wright D, Remoti L, Damvakeraki T, De Hert P, Papakonstantinou V, Beslay L, Dubois N (2014) EU Privacy Seals Project: Challenges and possible scope of an EU privacy seal scheme: Final report study deliverable 3.4. European Commission. http://bookshop.europa.eu/en/eu-privacy-seals-project-pbLBNA26699/downloads/LB-NA-26699-EN-N/LBNA26699ENN_002.pdf?FileName=LBNA26699ENN_002.pdf&SKU=LBNA26699ENN_PDF&CatalogueNumber=LB-NA-26699-EN-N. Accessed 1 July 2016

Rodrigues R, Wright D, Wadhwa K (2013) Developing a privacy seal scheme (that works). International Data Privacy Law, 3:100–116

Rouf I, Miller R, Mustafa H, Taylor T, Oh S, Xu W, Gruteser M, Trappe W, Seskar I (2010) Security and Privacy Vulnerabilities of In-Car Wireless Networks: A Tire Pressure Monitoring System Case Study. USENIX Security Symposium, 12 August 2010

Solove D (2008) Understanding Privacy. Harvard University Press, Cambridge, MA

Stanaland A, May L, Miyazaki D, (2011) Online Privacy Trust Marks: Enhancing the Perceived Ethics of Digital Advertising. Journal of Advertising Research, pp. 511–523

Stanley J, Crump C (2011) Protecting Privacy from Aerial Surveillance: Recommendations for Government Use of Drone Aircraft. ACLU, New York

Tranchard S (2013) Higher gear for standards and fully networked cars. ISO News. http://www.iso.org/iso/home/news_index/news_archive/news.htm?refid=Ref1716. Accessed 1 July 2016

TRUSTe (undated) TRUSTed Smart Grid Privacy Certification. https://www.truste.com/business-products/trusted-smart-grid/. Accessed 9 March 2016

Wolf C, Polonetsky J, Finch K (2015) A Practical Privacy Paradigm for Wearables. Future of Privacy Forum Whitepaper

Zittrain J (2006) The Generative Internet. Harvard Law Review 119. http://papers.ssrn.com/sol3/papers.cfm?abstract_id=847124. Accessed 1 July 2016

Chapter 8
An Economic Analysis of Privacy Seals

Patrick Waelbroeck

Contents

Patrick Waelbroeck, Professor of Industrial Economics and Econometrics, Telecom Paristech.
Email: patrick.waelbroeck@telecom-paristech.fr

P. Waelbroeck (✉)
Telecom Paristech, Paris, France
e-mail: patrick.waelbroeck@telecom-paristech.fr

© T.M.C. ASSER PRESS and the authors 2018   133
R. Rodrigues and V. Papakonstantinou (eds.), *Privacy and Data Protection Seals*,
Information Technology and Law Series 28, https://doi.org/10.1007/978-94-6265-228-6_8

Abstract This chapter proposes an economic analysis of privacy seals and trust-marks and their role in solving problems of information asymmetries that can reduce market participation. The chapter focuses on three aspects. First, the chapter analyses the demand for privacy protection and the supply of data protection and security. Second, the chapter provides an economic analysis of privacy seals. Finally, it discusses the economic impacts of privacy seals and trustmarks.

Keywords economic impact · privacy seals · trustmarks · business models · security · information asymmetries

8.1   Introduction

The digital economy is now "data-driven". Internet companies such as Amazon or Criteo use personal data to develop their business models based on product rec-ommendations and ad retargeting (see www.criteo.fr for a description of their business offers). Personal data can result from voluntary contributions (a consumer commenting on blog posts or assessing the quality of a product or the reputation of a seller) or involuntary traces (left by an Internet user in his navigation history). This raises the question of what types of data are being used by businesses and of what the risks for consumers are. Data used without the consent of a consumer can lead to negative externalities such as fraud, harassment, spam, hacking, identity theft, etc. Negative externalities arise from market failure when the actions of an economic agent exert a negative effect on other agents without compensation through a market mechanism. These risks are present at the data collection stage, at the data exploitation stage, and at the data transmission stage. Nevertheless, they are difficult to understand for the consumer. On the one hand, consumers find it difficult to verify how their personal data are being used by data collectors and processing organisations and it is difficult for them to know whether such use is legal or not. This is especially true in the big data era where independent datasets with little personal information can be combined rather easily to identify a person. On the other hand, an individual or consumer is hardly capable of assessing the level of IT security involved during different data processing stages. This leads to information asymmetry.

Information asymmetry arises when an economic agent has more information about the state of nature than another agent. It can lead to market breakdown. The economic impact of information asymmetries was first analyzed in the used-good markets where a seller knows the quality of the product that they sell better than the prospect, but has been applied to the labor and to financial markets. We can apply this concept to personal data, given that the company processing the data of its customers has more information about the legal compliance and the security of its IT infrastructure than the user. Companies themselves are not always in a position to fully assess the security of their information system: they sometimes do not even know if they have suffered a cyberattack. In this case, the integrity of the data system is unverifiable and the state of security and protection can be unknown to both the companies and the consumers.

Information asymmetry can encourage unscrupulous vendors (who do not comply with current regulations or good practice) to apply poor data protection policies, damaging the perceived quality of all products, and by extension reducing consumer market participation. In the presence of information asymmetries, consumers look for signals to assess the level of privacy, data protection and/or security of websites, products and services. Among these signals, privacy seals and trustmarks play a central role.

This chapter analyses the economic challenges associated with privacy seals and trustmarks. The chapter focuses on three aspects. First, the chapter analyses the demand for privacy protection and the supply of personal data protection and security. Second, the chapter provides an economic analysis of privacy seals, using insights from the other industries and highlighting new economic challenges. Finally, it discusses the economic impacts of privacy seals and trustmarks.

8.2   Understanding the Demand for Security and Personal Data Protection: The Sources of Negative Externalities

The main economic rationale for privacy protection is the existence of negative externalities for consumers. A negative externality arises when the action of an economic agent has a negative impact on another economic agent without a market mechanism to compensate for the disutility generated. Examples of negative externalities include:

- Identity fraud and identity theft that can happen when personal data are acquired without the consent of the individual
- Use of personal data by a third party for questionable purposes such as spamming or direct marketing
- Loss of personal data such as credit card numbers due to a lack of security of the servers where the data are stored.

Negative externalities (for the consumer) lead to too much data collected by companies compared to the social optimum. However, are market forces enough to force companies to protect personal data and the privacy of their clients? Acquisti (2004) argues that the market will not solve the problem of too much personal data collection if Internet users are not completely rational. He develops theories based on behavioral economics to show that it is easy to fool Internet users into giving away personal data by changing the design and the sequence of the web pages that they visit.

There are several factors that explain why consumers might want to protect their personal data—we review these next.

8.2.1 Price Discrimination

If businesses have more information about their clients and their behaviours, they can practice price discrimination: they can price the same product or service at different net prices. The net price includes net delivery and production costs. For digital products, the most widespread form of discrimination involves developing strategies to identify several consumer groups and proposing different versions of the same product or service to these groups. For example, a software manufacturer proposes different versions of the same product with different functions: a complete professional version and a basic (or student) version for which certain functions are unavailable. Personal information of consumers can therefore be used to customise offers for targeted customers, at often a very low cost for companies producing digital goods. Some consumers benefit from low prices, but others are charged higher prices and might decide to protect their personal data to avoid being price discriminated by using software to hide IP addresses, by using script blocking and other tools that make it harder for Internet companies to identify them.[1]

8.2.2 Targeting and Information Filters

Consumers receive information filtered by platforms such as Google or Amazon. For example, the Google search engine filters search results based on geo-localization, browsing history and ad profile. Amazon runs algorithms to deliver customised product recommendations based on a person's browsing history and purchases. Information filters can condition our behavior. They raise important economic issues mainly related to competition law. How can we ensure that consumers do not miss opportunities and that these filters do not reduce competition by excluding certain content, products or services? Who will guarantee that privacy protection tools will be offered to consumers?

Filter bubbles are created by algorithms that generate a unique universe for an Internet user that can potentially influence the way she or he thinks, behaves, and what she or he purchases. Again, some Internet users do not like to be influenced in such a way and find information filters a nuisance.[2]

---

[1] See the ACSE-CDC Baromètre de la confiance 2015: http://www.acsel.asso.fr/resultats-du-barometre-2015-acsel-cdc-de-la-confiance-des-francais-dans-le-numerique/. Accessed 16 January 2018.

[2] See Pariser 2011.

8.2.3   Ads (Ad-Adverse, Ad-Blockers)

Many online networks can be characterised by what economics literature calls 'two-sided markets'. They are illustrated by platforms characterised by network externalities between different groups of agents. For example, a search engine, such as Google.com, lets Internet users access content for free, and the site is funded by advertising. The site therefore matches advertisers with potential consumers. Consumers find the search more valuable when the number of targeted ads that they find are relevant. Similarly, an advertiser benefits from a large number of users who look for keywords on the platform and who come across targeted ads. There is therefore a positive externality between Internet users and advertisers. The dynamics of two-sided markets where internet users and advertisers interact implies that a small initial comparative advantage of a company can lead to its market domination through a positive feedback loop while platforms can be caught in a downward spiral. Thus, two-sided platforms can be highly concentrated.

The economic literature on advertising distinguishes two types of ads: informative and persuasive. Informative ads provide information on key product characteristics such as physical details, technical characteristics and prices. Persuasive ads are used to build a brand and do not necessarily provide useful information. While informative ads are valuable for a consumer, persuasive ads can be seen as a nuisance. Empirical work on the consumer perception of ads is scarce, but points to various attitudes, from ad-loving to ad-adverse.[3] These perceptions also vary from one country to the other. According to a study by Business Insider UK, one Internet user out of four uses an ad blocking tool in France, while only one out of ten in the US.[4]

8.2.4   Terms of Service Are Difficult to Read

It is important to have formal and written rules to address information asymmetries. A contract can be a way to address the questions of computer security and of the legal compliance of personal data protection. Terms of Service (ToS) are often used by companies selling digital products and services. However, as highlighted by Olurin et al. 2012; Anton et al. 2003, such ToS are are extremely difficult to read and to understand (McDonald and Cranor 2008; Becher and Tal 2015; Bakos et al. 2014). Moreover, they are always formulated in a take-it-or-leave-it offer i.e., the buyer of the product or the user of the service has to accept all conditions before

---

[3] See Anderson and Gabszewicz 2006.

[4] See http://uk.businessinsider.com/theres-some-new-data-out-on-the-huge-ad-blocking-trend-and-its-a-grim-read-for-online-publishers-2015-9. Accessed 1 September 2016.

using it. Upon analysing the economic impact of such contracts, we can conclude that terms of services that better protect personal data will lead to a lower level of profitability. On the one hand, data protection and security are costly to implement. On the other hand, terms of service that make it easier to exploit, re-use and sell personal data will generate more profits. A single contract for all users allows a company to make flexible rules with respect to personal data protection and is certainly not a guarantee for the user of the service that his or her personal data will be protected, thus creating and perpetuating further information asymmetries.

8.2.5 No Market Solution

The market cannot solve the structural problem of information asymmetries for three reasons. First, for an average consumer, the perceived benefits of a service largely exceeds the perceived costs resulting from an unauthorised access to his or her personal data. Second, consumers often lack the ability to critically assess the risks associated with their online behavior, which may partly reflect on poor awareness. For example, an Internet user often does not have the legal knowledge required to fully assess the compliance of the company's personal data policy to current regulations. An internet user may also not have the technical competence to assess the privacy protections offered by the company (if at all these are made available). Third, Gross and Acquisti 2005 identify a "Privacy Paradox" where they emphasise a sharp contrast between the stated intent of consumers which reflects a strong willingness to protect their personal data and a limited willingness to share their personal information online often reported in surveys, and their actual behavior online, where they share a lot of personal information without taking into consideration the risks that they initially acknowledged. This "paradox" should, nevertheless, be used with caution.

A study (Turow et al. 2015) found that people are aware of the risks of divulging personal data but are nonetheless resigned to giving up their data. Moreover, Andrade et al. (2002), provide a potential explanation for the privacy paradox. Using an experimental setup, they measure the sensitivity of the personal data being disclosed and they show that level of privacy concerns of laboratory participants doubles when one asks questions related to their online habits and when one asks questions about their identity. The "privacy paradox" ignores the difference in the nature of the personal data being shared and thus ignores data sensitivity. Thus it is possible to find that consumers do not seem to care about unimportant personal information such as their ZIP/post code, but that at the same time they protect they more sensitive information such as birthdate, religion or health status.

8.3   Understanding the Supply: Security as an Economic Good

We now study the factors that can influence the decisions of companies to secure their data infrastructure and to protect the personal data of their customers. In this chapter, we mainly review the factors that reduce the incentives for firm to secure their data infrastructure. First, security can be analysed as a public good for which there is underinvestment by the private sector. There are negative externalities associated with the lack of protection of personal data that are not compensated by market mechanisms. This can lead to situations in which customer data are at risk and exposed to leaks, fraud or theft. Second, companies develop business strategies to quickly reach a critical mass at the expense of securing their data infrastructure. Finally, data analytics and business intelligences often require firms to share personal data of their customers with third parties that do not necessarily have incentives to protect them. Information asymmetry in relation to the level of security of the data infrastructure make it easier for firms to share data without customers being aware of it.

8.3.1   Public Good

Public goods are non-rival and non-excludable.[5] These two characteristics imply that a single agent cannot capture the total surplus that he or she creates for the whole society. Indeed, in an ecosystem of companies sharing data, individual members benefit from the efforts of the other members who secure the system. Moreover, firms have therefore reduced incentives to secure the data of their customers compared to the social optimum because they do not take into account the negative externalities pointed out in Sect. 8.2. Overall, there will be underinvestment by the private sector and personal data in the ecosystem will be weakly protected.

8.3.2   Network Externalities

Moore and Anderson 2012 study the effect of network externalities on the level of security implemented by software makers. Positive network externalities arise when the value of the product or the service increases with the number of users. For instance, the value of a certain type of software increases with the number of its

---

[5] A non-rival good is a good whose consumption by one consumer does not prevent simultaneous consumption by other consumers. A good or service is non-excludable if non-paying consumers cannot be prevented from consuming it.

users, because it easier to exchange files with friends, colleagues and other contacts. It is therefore important for a firm, that wants to dominate this type of market, to quickly reach a critical mass. In this context, there are very few incentives to spend time and effort to secure personal data, because companies focus on reaching a critical mass. On the contrary, it is more profitable to let independent security experts find bugs and security holes and then fix the problems with software updates and patches.

8.3.3 Business Models Based on Data Exchange

When firms develop their business strategies based on ads, they generate revenues by selling the data of their customers to third parties. These firms have incentives to write very general Terms of Service to be able to make extensive use (and re-use) of their customers' data. When personal data are transferred to third parties, it is very difficult for a customer to determine how his or her data is being used, stored, and secured. Ad exchanges with real time bidding auctions exacerbate these problems, because personal data available in cookies are transmitted and matched by other platforms and third-party companies. Personal data can then be used without consent by firms that are remotely connected to the company's customers.

8.3.4 Data Lock-In

Increasing returns to scale in data storage and processing and the existence of positive indirect network externalities in multi-sided online platforms have created dominant Internet monopolies.[6] Internet users have few alternatives but to accept the terms and conditions of these firms. Moreover, the convenience of returning to a web site where personal information and contacts are stored and easily available creates situations of data or social lock-in, in which a user has a high cost of switching to a competitor.[7]

---

[6] Most Internet platforms are multi-sided with indirect positive externalities. For instance, Google and Facebook match advertisers and Internet users. The advertisers value more platforms where there are many Internet users (indirect positive externalities between the two sides of the platform). A platform that gains a slight initial advantage over its competitors benefits from a vicious circle that can lead to a dominant position.

[7] Mantelero 2013.

8.4   Economic Analysis of Privacy and Data Protection Seals

This section analyses the economic trade-offs of the formats, the institutional nature and the business models of privacy seals and trustmarks. A membership-based trustmark is delivered by an association to its members against a fee. It usually delivered by a private company e.g., TRUSTe in the US. A pubic trustmark is delivered by a public authority based on a regulation, law, or policy. A binary trustmark signals whether the company has reached a certain level of certification of compliance with existing regulations or charters. A continuous trustmark has several levels of compliance, usually represented by letters or colors.

8.4.1   Membership-Based Versus Public Trustmarks

A trustmark is less credible if it is based on voluntary membership for obvious reasons. The relationship between the organisation that delivers the seal or trustmark and its members is ambiguous. It is a "one principal-multiple agents" relationship where the members are also clients. The principal is interested in acquiring new clients has therefore less incentives to check the compliance of its clients with contractual standards. Hence, members protect the data of their customers only if they believe that the probability of getting caught is relatively high.

Who should control and audit the data infrastructure of the members of a trustmark or privacy seals programme? Companies or institutions delivering the trustmark or privacy seal should be responsible for the compliance of their prospects with respect to the standard of quality. Indeed, they build a capital of trust that they have interest in maintaining. Privacy seals and data protection trustmarks can only gain trust of their customers (the organisations that pay the fees) if the auditing process is reliable. Public and private trustmarks only differ in the way that they implement the auditing process, and will therefore be competing for customer acquisition.

As the basis for the grant of a trustmark or privacy seal, a standard provided by the government that is too low compared to industry best practices, loses its signaling power. Some companies would prefer to pay an additional cost to adopt a higher quality private seal in order to signal their higher quality to their customers and gain a competitive and reputational advantage. If government standards are close to those of high-quality companies, firms will rely on the public seal to signal the high quality of their personal data protection policy. Finally, if there are only public trustmarks, there is a risk of adverse selection that can lead to the exclusion of the highest quality firms if the standard is too low (or of the medium to high quality firms, if the standard is too high). Setting up the right level for the standard is therefore a critical element to take into consideration.

8.4.2   Formats: Continuous Versus Binary

There are mainly two formats of trustmarks that have different economic implications: continuous and binary. A continuous trustmark provides a range of different values, colors or signs (for instance letters).[8] A binary trustmark only signals whether the firm complies with the minimum standard of quality or not. Roe and Sheldon 2007 find that continuous trustmarks greatly reduce information asymmetries and result in prices and quality equivalent to those prevailing in a situation of perfect information. For binary trustmarks, there is a risk that the low quality standard will be preferred by low-income consumers and low standard companies, and that the high standards will be preferred by consumers with high income, buying from high standard companies.

8.4.3   Checking Compliance and Resolving Conflicts

Sometimes, the contract between the organisation that delivers the trustmark to its members specifies that the members pay to resolve conflicts with customers. Sometimes the customer has to pay in order to resolve the conflict. This could lead inefficiencies if the dispute resolution costs are high. For instance, Connolly 2008 demonstrated that enforcement action was rare against TRUSTe members. He provided many examples of privacy breaches between 1998 and 2007 (including breaches at AOL, Facebook, Hotmail, Microsoft and Real Networks) that were not followed by enforcement actions.

Recently, the US Federal Trade Commission (FTC) finalised its order against TRUSTe alleging that from 2006 to January 2013, TRUSTe failed to conduct annual re-certifications of companies holding TRUSTe privacy seals in over 1,000 incidences, despite representing on its website that companies holding TRUSTe Certified Privacy Seals receive recertification every year.[9]

It is obvious that a private seal without a strong audit policy will lose its signaling power for consumers.

8.4.4   Different Business Models: Pros and Cons

The next question is the fee charged by the organisation delivering the trustmark. On the one hand, a high fee of a trustmark excludes small companies from getting the certification. On the other hand, a high fee signals to consumers that the firm

---

[8] For an example, see Kelley et al. 2009.

[9] See the FTC press release available at https://www.ftc.gov/news-events/press-releases/2014/11/truste-settles-ftc-charges-it-deceived-consumers-through-its. Accessed 5 September 2016.

displaying the trustmark is financially strong and that it has enough resources to protect the personal data of its customers. A high fee reflects a high reputation of the organisation that delivers the trustmark and a high quality of the certification process. This argument is of course only valid if Internet users are aware of the fees paid by the companies running the websites that they are visiting.

A low fee does not let the trustmark play its role of signal and could lead to a limited budget for the company selling the trustmark in order to audit its members. A free certification is only possible if it is financed by a consortium or a public agency. The question of the cost associated with large scale free public data protection trustmarks and privacy seals is still unanswered.

8.5   Economic Impact (The Good, the Bad and the Ugly)

The economic evidence on the efficiency of trustmarks and privacy seals points to a small price increase and to a positive effect of sales, but also to risky consumer behavior induced by a misunderstanding of the underlying privacy and data protection policies. Overall, Miyazaki and Krishnamurthy 2002 found that 32% of all Fortune E-50 firms, nearly 5% of Fortune 500 firms, and 14% of Information Week 100 firms were TRUSTe or BBBOnLine licensees, the two main trustmarks in 2002. More recent studies point to similar numbers for the penetration of privacy seals and trustmarks among the most visited websites (roughly 7 out of 50).

8.5.1   Price Increase

Some studies show a significant price increase of a product manufactured by a company that adopts a food label. Kiesel and Villas-Boas 2007 find a price increase of about 40% for organic milk, Loureiro and McCluskey 2000 find a price increase of 22% for uncontaminated beef. On the real estate market, Brounen and Kok 2011 find a price increase of about 4% for an energy label. Mai et al. 2010 estimate that an e-commerce trustmark increases the price on the website by 1.5%. The difference between the different industries stems from the perceived risk. It is higher for food and health labels, lower for real estate and e-commerce trustmarks. A user will be more willing to pay a rate increase for a product if the risk associated with doubtful quality is critical. An additional problem arises on the Internet, because most services are given for free and financed by ads. It is hard to measure a price effect resulting from the adoption of a privacy seal.

The economic theory on reputation shows that a good reputation has economic value that is nevertheless difficult to measure. Indeed, reputation can be manipulated. A large number of studies show that there exist a positive but low reputation premium: firms with a good reputation (member of privacy seals program for instance) can charge a higher price than the market.[10]

8.5.2 Sales

Reputation increases the likelihood for a seller to finalise a transaction. For example, Cabral and Hortaçsu 2010 show that the number of negative evaluations on eBay.com leads to a decrease in the sale price. They also show that when a seller receives his or her first negative evaluation, his or her sales decrease by 13%. A seller who receives several negative evaluations is more likely to leave the e-commerce platform. Similarly, Bounie et al. 2012 show that there is a positive reputation premium that can reach 10% on Amazon Marketplace. Thus, active management of reputation has economic value and explains why it is important to maintain a display a privacy seal or a trustmark.

Garg et al. 2003 measure the impact of reputation on the market value of a company. They studied 22 computer attacks between 1996 and 2002, and show that a company stock market price declined by 2.7% on average in the day following the day of the attack. This drop increases to 4.5% on the third day after the attack. They distinguish four types of attack: alteration of the site, denial of service (DoS); theft of bank and customer information. It is worth noting that when financial information is involved, the stock price decreases by 9.3% on the same day and can reach 15% on the third day after the attack. Finally, the authors observed a positive correlation between the number of personal information that have been compromised, and the extent of impact.

8.5.3 Longevity and Timing Issues

Many privacy seals and trustmarks do not live very long and companies or institutions managing them can change their privacy certification policies, leading to confusion for the consumers about their value.[11] In addition, a website can adhere to a trustmark, or a privacy seal for some period, then interrupt its membership and finally join again later. What happens when the website is not certified is an open question. Connolly 2008 reports that the BBB Online Privacy Seal service at its peak had accredited over 700 websites. New applications ended in 2007 and the complete service (including managing complaints for existing accredited sites) ceased on 1 July 2008. Many sites still displayed the seal by the end of 2008. The author also notes that the biggest timing problem is the volatile nature of

---

[10] See Fan et al. 2016 for a recent contribution.
[11] For a discussion, see Rodrigues et al. 2013.

membership of trustmark schemes. Memberships often lapse for non-payment. Consumers lose their rights (or become confused about their rights) during the period where the membership is on hold but they are rarely aware of it.

8.5.4   Fake Signals, Wrong Interpretation of What Is Being Protected

Untrustworthy websites can use fake privacy seals to acquire new consumers and to generate business. Miyazaki and Krishnamurthy 2002 even argue that "the lack of participation by many popular online firms (e.g., Amazon.com, Buy.com, Travelocity, Ameritrade) may lead consumers to believe that only those firms with a need to externally validate their privacy practices will participate in Internet seal programs. This would imply that licensees may actually have worse online privacy practices than non-licensees."[12] They find no difference in privacy practice standards between firms participating to a seal program (such as Trustee or BBOnline) and other firms.

Thus, consumers could misinterpret what is protected compared to what they believe is protected. Furthermore, Miyazaki and Krishnamurthy 2002 find that a seal program enhances the perception of consumers with respect to privacy protection and might lead them to disclose more personal information. Consumers who believe that there are protected by a privacy seal might reveal more about themselves than without privacy seals.

Bellman et al. 2004 find that there are international differences in the perception of database errors and of secondary uses by third parties. There is a strong parallel between the perception of privacy protection and the regulatory regime (i.e., dictatorship, democracy, etc.) too.

8.6   Conclusion and Open Questions

This chapter analysed the demand for trustmarks by consumers as a means to solve information asymmetries about the state of protection of their personal data. Even though trustmarks reduce information asymmetries, there remain issues such as the misunderstanding of what is really protected that can lead to too much personal information disclosure. The chapter also argued that there are structural reasons to believe that without strong regulation, companies will underinvest in data protection and security.

A privacy program can be seen as a platform charging its members a fee and offering the label as a reward for display to the member's consumers. Finding the

---

[12] Miyazaki and Krishnamurthy 2002.

right business model will be challenging for institutions and organisations delivering trustmarks. Low fees for the members decrease the level of financial resources required for auditing. High fees lead to the risk that members become client and that small firms are excluded. Current privacy seals programs only count hundreds of members.[13] How to handle greater number of members, both technically and economically, will also be a key challenge in the future.

The next question is how to set the right number of seals/trustmarks. First, Hu et al. 2010 find that too many seals weaken the level of trusts of participants. Second, different public and private seals and trustmarks compete in the marketplace and setting the right level for the standard of quality of the certification program is a challenging task.

Finally, to define and assess the efficiency of privacy seals, analysts and academic researchers need to agree on the criteria to use: the costs-benefits for the applicant, the harm to consumers, the number of privacy breaches, the economic impact on the market, etc.

References

Acquisti A (2004) Privacy and security of personal information. Economics of Information Security, pp 179–186

Anderson S, Gabszewicw JJ (2006) The Media and Advertising: A Tale of Two-Sided Markets. In: Ginsburgh V, Throsby D (eds) The Handbook of the Economics of Art and Culture. North-Holland/Elsevier, pp 567–614

Andrade E B, Kaltcheva V, Weitz B (2002) Self-disclosure on the web: The impact of privacy policy, reward, and company reputation. Advances in Consumer Research 29(1):350–353

Anton A, Earp JB, Bolchini D, He Q, Jensen C, Stufflebeam W (2003) The lack of clarity in financial privacy policies and the need for standardization. IEEE Security & Privacy, 2(2):36–45

Bakos Y, Marotta-Wurgler F, Trossen DR (2014) Does Anyone Read the Fine Print? Consumer Attention to Standard Form Contracts. New York University Law and Economics Working Paper 195

Becher SI, Tal Z (2015) Online Consumer Contracts: No One Reads, But Does Anyone Care? Jerusalem Review of Legal Studies, forthcoming

Bellman S, Johnson EI, Kobrin SJ, Lohse GL (2004) International Differences in Information Privacy Concerns: A Global Survey of Consumers. Information Society 20 (5):313–324

Bounie D, Eang B, Sirbu M, Waelbroeck P (2012) Online price dispersion: An International Comparison. Working paper

Brounen D, Kok N (2011) On the economics of energy labels in the housing market. Journal of Environmental Economics and Management 62(2):166–179

Cabral L, Hortaçsu A (2010) The dynamics of seller reputation: The case of eBay. Journal of Industrial Economics 58:54–78

Connolly C (2008) Trustmark Schemes Struggle to Protect Privacy. Working paper

Fan Y, Ju J, Xiao M (2016) Reputation premium and reputation management: Evidence from the largest e-commerce platform in China. International Journal of Industrial Organization 46

---

[13] Connolly 2008.

Garg A, Curtis J, Halper H (2003) Quantifying the financial impact of IT security breaches. Information Management & Computer Security, 11(2):74–83

Gross R, Acquisti A (2005) Information revelation and privacy in online social networks. Proceedings of the 2005 ACM workshop on Privacy in the electronic society. ACM, New York, pp 71–80

Hu H, Xu J, On ST (2010) Privacy-Aware Location Data Publishing. Transactions on Database Systems (TODS) 35(3)

Kelley PG, Bresee J, Cranor LF, Reeder RW (2009) A "Nutrition Label" for privacy. In: Proceedings of the 5th Symposium on Usable Privacy and Security, p. 4. ACM, New York

Kiesel K, Villas-Boas SB (2007) Got organic milk? Consumer valuations of milk labels after the implementation of the USDA organic seal. Journal of agricultural & food industrial organization 5(1)

Loureiro ML, McCluskey JJ (2000) Consumer preferences and willingness to pay for food labeling: A discussion of empirical studies. Journal of Food Distribution Research 34(3):95–102

Mai B, Menon NM, Sarkar S (2010) No free lunch: Price premium for privacy seal-bearing vendors. Journal of Management Information Systems 27(2):189–212

Mantelero A (2013) Competitive value of data protection: The impact of data protection regulation on online behavior. International Data Privacy Law 3(4): 229–238

McDonald A, Cranor L (2008) The Cost of Reading Privacy Policies. I/S: A Journal of Law and Policy for the Information Society

Miyazaki AD, Krishnamurthy S (2002) Internet seals of approval: Effects on online privacy policies and consumer perceptions. The Journal of Consumer Affairs 28–49

Moore T, Anderson R (2012) Internet security. In: The Oxford Handbook of the Digital Economy. Oxford University Press

Olurin M, Adams C, Logrippo L (2012) Platform for privacy preferences (p3p): Current status and future directions. IEEE, Tenth Annual International Conference on Privacy, Security and Trust (PST), pp 217–220

Pariser E (2011) The Filter Bubble: What the Internet is Hiding From You. Penguin Press, UK

Rodrigues R, Barnard-Wills D, Wright D, De Hert D, Papakonstantinou V (2013) EU Privacy Seals Project: Inventory and analysis of privacy certification schemes. European Commission Joint Research Centre Institute for the Protection and Security of the Citizen, Final Report

Roe B, Sheldon I (2007) Credence good labeling: The efficiency and distributional implications of several policy approaches. American Journal of Agricultural Economics 89(4):1020–1033

Turow J, Hennessy M, Draper N (2015) The Trade-Off Fallacy: How Marketers are Misrepresenting American Consumers and Opening Them Up to Exploitation. Report. Annenberg School for Communication, University of Pennsylvania

Chapter 9
Conclusion: What Next for Privacy Seals?

Rowena Rodrigues

Contents

Abstract Based on the chapters in this book, this chapter looks afresh at the position, role and future of privacy seals. It presents a brief SWOT (strengths, weaknesses, opportunities, threats) analysis, and presents some hallmarks of a quality privacy and/or data protection seal.

Keywords privacy seals · data protection seals · privacy certification · SWOT · GDPR

Privacy seals are at a crossroads. Where previously their role and direction were relatively clear, they now face a challenging future with multiple directions they could take, based on technological developments, regulatory stimuli (particularly in

Rowena Rodrigues is a Senior Research Analyst at Trilateral Research Ltd. e-mail: rowena. rodrigues@trilateralresearch.com. Trilateral Research Ltd., Crown House, 72 Hammersmith Road, London W14 8TH, UK.

R. Rodrigues (✉)
Trilateral Research Ltd., Crown House, 72 Hammersmith Road, London W14 8TH, UK
e-mail: rowena.rodrigues@trilateralresearch.com

© T.M.C. ASSER PRESS and the authors 2018
R. Rodrigues and V. Papakonstantinou (eds.), *Privacy and Data Protection Seals*,
Information Technology and Law Series 28, https://doi.org/10.1007/978-94-6265-228-6_9

the EU), and industry demand (or lack of it). Let us briefly recap and analyse the state of affairs, and where privacy seals might go from here.

9.1 Strengths

Privacy seals continue to be an easily accessible and visible, demonstrable means of providing information, or 'stamps of approval'[1] signifying adherence to privacy standards, criteria or requirements. CNIL (the French data protection authority) refers to them as a "confidence indicator".[2] As Rodrigues et al. state, "privacy seals have an innate ability to easily and quickly present an entity's privacy and data protection commitments."[3] With ever increasing complexities in the nature of online and offline transactions and hidden, yet escalating impacts on privacy (and personal data of individuals), privacy seals might still be a good tool (and/or a quick and easy means) to help individuals and entities develop a positive attitude and loyalty towards a brand, product or service that adopts good privacy and/or data protection practices. As Hansen states, "The mere existence of the seal demonstrates to users that the providers take their privacy seriously and are willing to invest in data protection and security."[4]

9.2 Weaknesses

But privacy seals have their weaknesses. Their ability to function as 'credible' signals of privacy adherence is only as good as their underlying criteria, their monitoring, and their enforcement. The successful ability of a privacy seal to perform its role, is also affected by the identity of its issuer—e.g., a seal issued by a long established and trusted organisation, or data protection authority, will have much more credibility than one that is issued by a newly established certification organisation or by a non-trustworthy organisation. Privacy seal issuers (or certifiers) themselves might compromise a certification scheme—e.g., through conflicts of interest (bias towards applicants), inactive scheme elements, not devoting (adequate) resources to monitoring, enforcing and reviewing certifications, lack of transparency (poorly accessible scheme details, no complaints mechanisms) etc.

The nature of privacy seals makes them highly susceptible to abuse e.g., counterfeiting of seals, wrongful use (e.g., use of a seal beyond period of certification).

---

[1] Information Commissioner's Office 2015.

[2] CNIL 2017.

[3] Rodrigues et al. 2013.

[4] Hansen 2009.

The more successful a privacy seal, the more likely it is that such seals would become susceptible to misuse in unauthorised manners. This is very harmful as individuals relying on a seal as a visible reassurance cannot often determine at a quick glance, the authenticity of the seal. Privacy seals can also mislead—i.e., due to the variety of certification schemes in existence, as Waelbroeck points out "there remain issues such as the misunderstanding of what is really protected".[5]

A privacy seal might also give off wrong signals; a seal is only as good as the criteria and requirements it signifies are being met. A seal might have been awarded for a bare minimal level of privacy adherence but this might not be evident to individuals who rely on the seal (and might misleadingly think that the seal is a very good privacy guarantee) and want a quick reassurance their privacy is being respected. The wide variety of seals in existence with different criteria and requirements (technical, legal, good practice or a mix-and-match of the three) as their underlying basis, still poses a significant challenge to whether seals are a good privacy protection measure.

9.3 Opportunities

Technologies and innovations are posing constant challenges for privacy. Will privacy seals still be relevant in the face of the shifting of privacy norms and expectations, and the shifting of the natures of technologies (i.e., autopoietic,[6] disruptive, distributed, creative, hyper-connected, immersive, ubiquitous)? Some contexts explored in the book (e.g., Chap. 7 on the potential for privacy seals in emerging technologies) illustrate this: cyber-physical technologies, smart cars, and smart homes. The conclusion drawn is that for a privacy seal to "work" in the contexts it seeks to operate, it might be more feasible to "assert certain specific patterns of digital and organisation behaviour". But might privacy seals and/or certification work in other contexts too? For example, printable organs, created for transplantation or replacement in the human body are going to become much more common in the future. The computer-aided design (CAD) files and 3D replicas of the organs may create privacy and data protection vulnerabilities and risks[7] as they may contain personal data, consent might be absent, and it could be shared in a risky manner with third parties. Here, there might be an opportunity to certify the organisations offering bioprinting, or the bioprinting devices. Another opportunity presents in the form of Internet-connected toys (that have received and are receiving severe negative publicity for privacy-invasive practices (e.g., recording children's voices and storing their data).[8] A privacy and data protection seal (potentially, in connection with the CE marking) for internet-connected toys could help provide

---

[5] See Chap. 8.

[6] Brian 2009.

[7] Coraggio 2015.

[8] Claburn 2016; Bray 2016; Brady 2016.

much needed reassurances that privacy and data protection standards and requirements have been adhered to.

In the EU, the General Data Protection Regulation (GDPR) provides a definitive
encouragement to data protection certification mechanisms, seals and marks.
The GDPR has created an opportunity for national supervisory authorities, the
European Data Protection Board (EDPB) and the European Commission to get their
foot firmly wedged in the door of a previously, largely industry-led exclusive club that
(still) views privacy seals as an industry-led, self-regulatory tool. One can see an
opportunity here for privacy seals to increasingly become more of a co-regulatory tool.
Cavoukian and Chibba particularly highlight that "privacy seals could come into their
own as a powerful facilitator of globalization of consumer transactions if they are able to
provide acceptable and enforceable privacy protection across multiple jurisdictions".[9]

If one looks back into history and particularly at seals (e.g., those used by royals, the
papacy, or blacksmiths), the destruction of seals when authority was passed on
enhanced the importance of such seals as means of authentication. This does not
happen in the case of contemporary privacy seals, and is perhaps a lost opportunity.
While terminating or repudiating bad privacy seal schemes was not possible (or heard
of) in the previously self-regulated privacy seals market, maybe with the increasing
regulatory interest in this sector (at least in the EU), there is a potential for privacy seal
schemes that do not pass muster (e.g., those that collude with seal applicants to provide
lax certification or that are a sham) to be acted against and even taken down—this
would be a big step forward not only in safeguarding the interests of parties that rely on
privacy seals but also in safeguarding the future of privacy seals sector itself.

9.4 Threats

As recognised by Balboni and Dragan,[10] there are still practical and regulatory
barriers that impede the success of privacy seals (though these are not insur-
mountable). The threats include: the environment in which they operate (the
presence of a large number of diversified seal types has resulted in extreme fragmentation), the status afforded to them (the ones that certify legal requirements and
are issued by data protection authorities would have a definite advantage over seals
issued by private, commercial entities that have determined the criteria for certification on the basis of industry practice—whether it is good practice or otherwise),
bad press (e.g., privacy snake oil,[11] malware lurking behind safety seals).[12] Kamara
and De Hert[13] particularly highlight that "the lack of maturity of the (data

---

[9] Chapter 5.

[10] Chapter 6.

[11] Stevens 2014.

[12] Leyden 2006.

[13] Chapter 2.

protection) certification market, the data protection authorities in terms of relevant expertise and resources, and the newly established European Data Protection Board, would not allow a wide adoption of the European Data Protection Seal or at least full development of the potential of such a strong pan-European seal operated by public authorities". Such threats cause (and pose) severe harm to the desirability of privacy seals. Some of these threats could, and should be addressed by the regulatory and policy measures to support good privacy seal schemes. Other threats need a more targeted approach if they are to be effectively addressed. The industry and public media are good platforms that should be channelled to counter the vilification of privacy seals.

9.5   The Hallmarks of a Quality Privacy and/or Data Protection Seal

Based on the previous literature on the topic, and the analysis presented in this book, here are some key questions that can help distinguish between a good and bad privacy and/or data protection seal:

- Does the privacy and/or data protection seal certification minimise privacy and/or data protection risks? Does it support the privacy/data protection compliance?
- Is the scope of the seal clear? What exactly does it certify i.e., a product, a service, a system, an organisation?
- Is the issuer of the privacy seal/certifier a reliable and trusted entity? Is the issuer accredited? (Reliability of the issuer is critical to engendering trust and reputation of the seal)
- Is the certification based on (clear and transparent) criteria (derived either from law, or industry and/or sectoral standards, codes and guidance)?
- Is the privacy and/or data protection seal verifiable (either by looking it up on an up-to-date list, register or website)?
- Does the privacy and/or data protection seal issuer monitor compliance post-issue of the seal?
- Can a breach of the certification conditions or misuse of the seal be reported?
- Is there a clear complaints process in place to deal with any complaints?

These are some key questions that can help determine whether a privacy and/or data protection seal is up to the mark. They can be asked of any type of seal, and by both applicants for privacy seals and individuals or entities that might seek to rely on the assurances that seals provide.

9.6   Privacy 'Pass', or Privacy 'Flunk'?

So, where do we go from here?

Privacy and/or data protection seals are here to stay (at least for the near future); their nature and function may dramatically change due to the pressures of, and the changes in the environments (human and technological) they operate in. Overall, the future for privacy seals is both promising, and tough, depending on some critical factors.

One factor is whether new privacy and data protection seal schemes can learn from the good and bad experiences of their predecessors. If they continue to be viewed and used only as marketing gimmicks by the industry, then their future is bleak.

Another factor is whether they will continue to hold their reputation as 'badges of honour'; this is something that is critical to their ability to flourish, perform their function (encourage and reward good privacy and data protection practices) and be competitive assets? If the wrong sort of privacy seals flourish, or for some reason the seals offered are brought into disrepute, their reputation will be severely affected. It will also affect the ability of seal schemes to draw subscribers as the proliferation of bad seals might negatively impact the ability of companies with good privacy seals to gain competitive or reputational advantages.

Another factor is whether existing schemes can adapt sufficiently well to the demands of the new fluid environments (i.e., technological, regulatory and societal) they will operate in. Privacy and data protection seals need to be robust and yet dynamic. If not, they will fade into oblivion and something new take their place e.g., privacy pass or fail registries (or blacklists) for products and services that are privacy- unfriendly or do not meet legal and other established privacy and data protection standards; product/service/system privacy warranties, or a privacy footprint of sorts?

The future for privacy and data protection seals depends on whether they can learn from the past. In addition to whether they are optimised to perform well (through regulatory, financial and industry support), two critical elements for their success will continue to be: whether they can communicate well and whether they can continue to engender trust.

References

Brady K (2016) Internet capable 'spy' toys put data protection and child safety at risk. DW. http://www.dw.com/en/internet-capable-spy-toys-put-data-protection-and-child-safety-at-risk/a-36674091. Accessed 20 March 2017

Bray H (2016) Could your children's toys be violating their privacy? Boston Globe. https://www.bostonglobe.com/business/2016/12/06/nuance-under-fire-over-toy-privacy/WryFiVdq6zIVTxLuRImdVI/story.html. Accessed 20 March 2017

Brian A W (2009) The Nature of Technology. Free Press, New York

Claburn T (2016) Playtime's over: Internet-connected kids toys 'fail miserably' at privacy. The Register. http://www.theregister.co.uk/2016/12/08/connected_toys_fail_miserably_at_privacy/. Accessed 20 March 2017

CNIL (2017) Privacy seals. https://www.cnil.fr/en/privacy-seals. Accessed 20 March 2017

Coraggio G (2015) Top 3 legal issues of 3D Printing! Technology's Legal Edge. https://www.technologyslegaledge.com/2015/09/top-3-legal-issues-of-3d-printing/. Accessed 20 March 2017

Hansen M (2009) Putting Privacy Pictograms into Practice - A European Perspective. In: Fischer S, Maehle E, Reischuk R (eds) Proceedings of GI Jahrestagung. Bonn, Gesellschaft für Informatik (GI), pp 1703–1716

Information Commissioner's Office (2015) Privacy seals. https://ico.org.uk/for-organisations/improve-your-practices/privacy-seals/. Accessed 20 March 2017

Leyden J (2006) Malware lurks behind the seal: A question of TRUSTe. The Register. http://www.theregister.co.uk/2006/09/26/truste_privacy_seal_row/. Accessed 20 March 2017

Rodrigues R, Barnard-Wills D, Wright D, De Hert P, Papakonstantinou V (2013) EU Privacy Seals Project: Inventory and analysis of privacy certification schemes. Final Report Study Deliverable 1.4. Publications Office of the European Union, Luxembourg

Stevens T (2014) Privacy Seals and Privacy Snake Oil. ComputerWeekly.com. http://www.computerweekly.com/blog/Identity-Privacy-and-Trust/Privacy-Seals-and-Privacy-Snake-Oil. Accessed 20 March 2017